COMPENDIUM

Spiritual Care through Muslim Ethnographic Stories

Harvard Shuttle and the Sufi

Volume 1

Dr. Yunus Kumek

Sage Chronicle λ
publishing house

Cover image: Unsplash.com

Sage Chronicle $^\lambda$
p u b l i s h i n g   h o u s e

www.sagechronicle.org
3380 Sheridan Drive, #240
New York 14226
contact@sagechronicle.org

ISBN 978-1-951050-21-4

Published in the United States of America.

PREFACE

This book brings into our contemporary life important Muslim teachings in a one-page story format. Each story has the first paragraph as the story and the second paragraph as the meanings and interpretations of the practice. The stories in the book aim to use contemporary life encounters with the meanings and interpretations in Islamic practice. These stories have been compiled and contemporized from ethnographic field work in different Sufi communities of New York, Boston, Pittsburgh, Chicago, Toronto, Istanbul, and Cairo.

The book uses a simple transliteration scheme from the original language of Arabic without going to the details of academic transliteration scheme. When there are names or referrals to God then the words are capitalized such as the Divine. The abbreviation used for the Prophet Muhammad is the Prophet. The footnotes with numbered superscripts give the immediate relevant information for the unfamiliar English reader. The endnotes with lettered superscripts give the information for the reader who is familiar with the teachings and readings in Sufism. The references with numbered and parenthesis superscripts allude to the notions in practice as some examples of these practices in the literature. The suggested readings are examples of some classical and contemporary work about the topic for interested readers. The glossary and index in the book can hopefully make it easier for general readers of English.

The short stories and anecdotes in this book can bring important and practical aspects of these teachings in our practical life. This book can be valuable for different level readers such as the Muslims, Christians, Jews, Buddhists, Hindus, and people who especially value spirituality and experiential knowledge and believe the mysteries of life beyond the seen and human control. Regardless of different naming of the deity as Allah, God, Adonai, or the notions of Nirvana or Samadhi, in this book, one can realize the similarity of common and intersecting points of spirituality or religious experience among different traditions.

The word "Sufi" or character of "Sufi" does not imply a group or sect in this case, but used to depict a self-reflective personality or a character trying to have a spiritual Muslim care in daily practices. So, each time you see the Sufi character, you can imagine and replace it with a "Muslim". It was also easy for me especially for Western audience just to denote everything as one character as Muslim without changing genders and trying to find 500 different Muslim gender names in more than 500 stories.

This book can be a valuable supplementary text in the disciplines of psychology, counseling, anthropology, philosophy, and religion.

Yunus Kumek, PhD
Lecturer in Muslim Ministry
Harvard Divinity School
Fall 2022

CONTENTS

COMPENDIUM

Spiritual Care through Muslim Ethnographic Stories

Harvard Shuttle and the Sufi

1.   The Sufi and the Upside Down Bug

One day, the Sufi was out for a walk with his children. As they walked, the Sufi was in deep thought. Then, the Sufi observed a bug struggling to regain its upright position. The Sufi continued walking. After a mile, the Sufi felt uneasy. He asked himself, "What is going on?" Then, he considered the bug and realized he should have helped it. After several minutes of searching, he returned to the initial location and found the insect still attempting to change its position. The Sufi turned the bug on its back. Afterwards, he felt much better and left.

IN PRACTICE

It is important to detect, diagnose, and treat one's spiritual problems accordingly. A lot of times, people may not know the cause of spiritual discomfort, uneasiness, fear, anxiety, or distress. By ignoring or mistreating issues, they can make matters worse. In practice, the famous saying "know yourself to know Allah ﷻ"[1] refers to this concept. Perhaps the Sufi in the story was distracted while thinking and walking with his children. When he saw the bug, he did not internalize the creature's pain. However, the image remained in his mind and changed into a sense of discomfort within himself. As the Sufi reflected on his discomfort, he came to the realization that his indifference toward the suffering bug was the cause of his distress.

Discussion Question

- ► How can one practice awareness of their surroundings in order to become more in tune with their emotions?
- ► How can one practice awareness to be more alert to others' suffering/feelings?

2.   The External, the Internal, and the Purpose

On a dark and rainy day, the Sufi went to a social club. As he went inside, he noticed the building's lighting was bright and everyone was cheerful. People were drinking coffee and enjoying conversations at every corner. They appeared to be well-dressed, content, and smiling. Then, he thought about his solitude, loneliness, and silence. He reflected on moments spent in the temple, mosque, or places of meditation. He asked himself, "What is the difference?" And answered, "This is the external. I don't know what these people are like when they are alone or in silence, and what are their real-selves and purpose.

In practice

It is essential to understand that internal engagements are the essence of one's life purpose. This does not mean that a person must be in gloomy environments to engage in prayers, chants, meditation, and reflection. As in the story above, a person can find happiness in a cheerful environment like the social club. One should be aware that the the universe is a social club if one knows how to engage with it.[2]. In other words, we live in a system where beings can appreciate one another's presence in position to Allah ﷻ. In this sense, people who do not recognize their position to Allah may not have a genuine purpose, even if they appear content. For those lacking self-reflection, there may be internal troubles such as depression, anxiety, and unhappiness.

Discussion Question

> ▶   How do you determine your real-self?

3.   Friend or Companion

One day, the Sufi contemplated the difference between a companion and friend. She thought to herself, "A companion is someone you spend time with. A friend is a person you invest in and have a closer relationship with."

IN PRACTICE

It is important to select one's companions and friends carefully. The presence of others can have a positive or negative effect on a person's spirituality. For instance, those who surrounded Rasulullah ﷺ were known as companions, or sahabah. They spent as much time as possible with Rasulullah ﷺ in order to receive the positive spiritual flow into their hearts and minds. Another Arabic word, sohbah, is derived from the same root as sahabah. Sohbah can mean "hang out" and "conversation." Together, these words point to the purpose of a companion as someone to hang around and converse with. On the other hand, Allah proves to be the greatest example of friendship in one's life, or the Khalil.[1] In this friendship, Allah will always be present and close if the individual reciprocates.[3]

Discussion Question

- ► How do you understand the difference between a companion and friend?
- ► How do you contextualize the definitions of companion and friend in present society?

----

1. Khalil is from khullah, genuine love and companionship.

4.   Life, Purpose, Worries, and the Sufi

One day, the Sufi was worried about getting older. She was particularly concerned about her life purpose. As she reflected, the Sufi did not feel good about the things she wanted to accomplish. She thought to herself, "I'm going to die soon. So, what should I do?" She searched her heart and said, "I will carry out intentions to do good as best as I can."

IN PRACTICE

People suffer from a common spiritual ailment known as forgetfulness of death.[2] This is typically due to the desire to live a long life. Nonetheless, it is essential to prepare for death. Preparing for death is not limited to external preparations such as drafting a will or arranging a funeral. It also includes internal preparations such as arranging intentions, efforts, and spiritual conflict in relationship with Allah. In the story above, the Sufi realizes that as she gets older she wants to work toward achieving the goals she had previously failed to accomplish[4]. Allah rewards a person for their good intentions and sincere efforts, not for the results of their intentions and efforts.

Discussion Question

 ▸ How or why do our concerns change as we age?
 ▸ What can you do to live the best as you can as you get older?

---

2. Tul-u amal: desire for long life.

5.   Balancing Ascetic Life and Social Life

One day, the Sufi was taking much pleasure in prayer. As he was praying, his mother called him for a moment of assistance. The Sufi stopped praying immediately and went to his mother. His mother was satisfied with him. The Sufi thought to himself, "Even though it was hard to break my prayer, if it pleases Allah, I will do it."

IN PRACTICE

The Prophet discourages[5] asceticism that detaches an individual from familial and social obligations. In other words, asceticism can be practiced for the purpose of self-improvement, either through prolonged solitude or temporary retreats. They can then return to the company of others, which is beneficial for both the individual and the community. There are a great number of authentic Sufi teachers who prefer to pray and meditate on Allah ☙ while in solitude. However, they also interact with members of the community, such as family and students. In the story above, the relationship between the Sufi and his mother illustrates how a person must cease their optional spiritual engagement if a member of their family or another close member of their community calls. By not adhering to this calling, as advised by the Prophet[1], pious people fail to maintain these familial and social ties, and Allah tests them with trials and tribulations.

Discussion Question

- ▶ Is ascetic life uncommon in today's age? Why?
- ▶ How might you live out an ascetic life as suggested by the Prophet?

6.   Mother Sufi

One day, the Sufi pondered why his children were more attached to their mother than to him. Then, he reflected on all the difficulties his wife endured during labor and with breastfeeding. She was constantly worried about taking care of the children. The Sufi thought to himself, "I think, I understand, it is a time to give back."

IN PRACTICE

According to the custom, both father and mother have parental rights over their children. In order to please Allah ﷻ, children are also expected to treat their parents with respect and courtesy, even if they do not get along well with them. The practice encourages children to be especially kind to their mothers. According to some interpretations of the Prophet, mothers[5] [6] have three times as many parental rights as fathers. This instruction is repeated numerous times in both the scripture and the Prophet's sayings[6][5].

Discussion Question

> ► What are the factors that affect parent–children relationship?

7.   Sufis from Different Cultures and Learning

There was a Sufi who would choose Sufis from various cultures as his friends. He spent each day with a Sufi from a different culture, including American, Indian, African, Turkish, and Arab Sufis. One of his friends recognized this and asked why. The Sufi stated, "I learn something new and different from each of them." They all interpret and practice being close to Allah ﷻ in similar yet distinct ways.

IN PRACTICE

On the spiritual path, the individual can benefit from the diverse perspectives of others. A person who may not have extensive knowledge but is skilled in practice can provide alternative viewpoints. A person with extensive knowledge but little practice can also provide unique perspectives. Similar spiritual teachings can have distinct meanings for each culture. As described in the story above, learning spiritual practices from people of different cultures is a very unique experience.

Discussion Question

- Why do some people view cultural diversity as beneficial to learning?
- Why might others see cultural diversity as a problem?

8.   Some Things Aren't Always as They Seem

Every day, a Sufi would drink coffee from a paper cup. One day, as usual, she took a paper cup from its package to pour the coffee, but it looked different from the other paper cups. "Perhaps this is a special paper cup," the Sufi thought to herself. "Perhaps it will last longer than the others." When she poured the coffee into the cup, she began screaming. The coffee was dripping from the bottom of the cup. "Good-seeming evils!" exclaimed the Sufi.

In practice

It is critical to understand that what appears to be good can actually be evil in its essence[7]. On the other hand, an evil-seeming incident can be beneficial to a person. As a result, as mentioned in the above story, one should not be misled by how something seems.

Discussion Question

- ▶ What is your experience with evil-seeming or good-seeming incidents?

9. Sufi's Promotion

A Sufi was working in a company and wanted to speak with her boss about a promotion. She asked her boss for a promotion one day, just before Thanksgiving. Her boss was in a good mood because Thanksgiving was approaching. When the Sufi received her promotion, she said, "Alhamdulillah, Thank you Allah ﷻ."

IN PRACTICE

Allah ﷻ is always merciful and forgiving, and he values repentance and gratitude. There are also times when Allah ﷻ shows special favor on people. During these times, Allah ﷻ[8] especially fulfills prayers, requests, and needs.

Discussion Question

- ▶ How can one implement wisdom before making requests at specific times/occasions?

10.   The No Wife-No Life Man and the Sufi

There was a man in the mosque who frequently complained to the Sufi, stating, "No wife, no life!" This individual was unable to marry. He frequently grumbled about his life, his brothers, and his poverty. Every day, the same event occurred. One day, another poor man was found sleeping in the mosque. This man with 'no wife and no life' returned to the Sufi and stated, "If I had money and a car, I could have assisted this poor man. However, I have nothing. What should I do?" The Sufi felt sorry for the man.

IN PRACTICE

It is important to have empathy for others, despite the fact that it can be challenging at times. Only Allah ﷻ knows the true circumstances of every individual. One of the constant prayers Sufis offer to Allah ﷻ is, "Oh Allah ﷻ, show us the realities of the world." In other words, something that appears to be bad may actually be good for the individual, while something that appears to be good may actually be bad for the individual.

Discussion Question

> ► Is it easy or difficult to sympathize with people? Why?

11.   Life, Pain, and the Gain

One day, the Sufi observed an elderly man weeping and praying in the mosque. The Sufi was familiar with the man. The man had no relatives or family members. He was scheduled for major surgery the following day. The Sufi exerted great effort not to cry at this scene. The Sufi then thought to himself, "Allah is more merciful than I or anyone else. There is suffering, but insha'Allah there is always gain if done with a pure heart."

IN PRACTICE

Sometimes, evil or tragic-appearing events can break our hearts. Occasionally, a memory or a negative experience can cause our hearts to hurt. One should remember to use every opportunity to strengthen one's relationship with Allah, whether it involves evil or good. This is the ultimate action that will result in rewards in this world and the afterlife. In the above story, the old man transformed his pain into a fruitful relationship of attachment and going back to Allah ﷻ and crying. Rasulullah ﷺ mentions that the power of tears genuinely flow in relationship of Allah ﷻ. The fire of hell cannot touch these eyes in the afterlife [9].

Discussion Question

> ▸ Why is it important to call on Allah in times of trouble?

12. Meanings, Feelings, Intention, and the Sufi

The Sufi did not feel well one day. She was contemplating the purpose of her life and death. She thought about her loved ones who had died, but it did not make her feel better. She engaged in more self-reflection. She asked herself, "What is troubling me?" Once she found the reason, she thought, "I've identified my life's purpose and the things that I was unable to achieve. At least, I made the intention."

IN PRACTICE

It is essential to have high goals, a desire to do good in life, and to please Allah ﷻ. On the path to Allah ﷻ, doing good comes with worship, practice, and learning. There are afterdeath narrations in the Qur'an and from Rasulullah ﷺ in which the deceased person begs Allah ﷻ for a second chance at life in order to do more good. But once a person dies, there is no return. According to this interpretation, the Sufi in the preceding story was experiencing feelings of self-responsibility and self-reflection. In the end, Allah ﷻ rewards the intent behind a person's character, even if the individual was unable to accomplish what he or she intended.

Discussion Question

 ▸ Why is the regular practice of self-reflection important?

13. The Disputing Sufi

One day, there was a Sufi who had a disagreement with her spouse. She believed that she was correct and held a grudge. However, she felt uneasy after the argument and asked her husband for forgiveness. She then felt better and more at ease.

IN PRACTICE

It is important not to have any ill feelings towards another person. Rasulullah ﷺ mentions that one cannot enter Heaven until one removes these feelings from one's heart[5][6]. In this perspective, the Sufi implemented this teaching and felt better.

Discussion Question

- ▸ How can carrying negative feelings for others hurt the person having these feelings?

14. The Old Sufi's Struggle

An elderly Sufi used to visit the mosque to pray. One day it rained, making the roads muddy. While walking slowly due to age-related physical issues, he slipped and fell in a mud puddle. Then, he returned to his home, changed his clothes, and returned to the mosque. Satan observed the Sufi. As the Sufi returned to the mosque, he once more slipped and fell in a mud puddle. Then, he returned and changed his clothes before returning to the mosque. Satan continued to observe the Sufi. Then, for the third time, he was about to fall into a mud puddle. Satan came to the man in human form came and helped him avoid falling. The old Sufi expressed gratitude and asked, "May I know your name?" He then declared, "I am Satan." The old man said: "Why did you help me?" He replied, "The first time you fell, you went home to change your clothes and then returned with great difficulty." Allah ﷻ forgave all of your sins as a result of your sincerity and effort. The second time you fell, you returned home to change and returned with great difficulty. Allah ﷻ forgave the sins of your entire family due to your sincere intent and efforts. As you left your home for the final time, I feared that Allah ﷻ would pardon everyone because of your sincere effort. Therefore, I wanted to assist you in going to the mosque to prevent this from occurring."

In practice

It is important to remember that the struggle is more important than the outcome according to Allah ﷻ. If one has the right intention and struggle as a result, then the person is using the right vehicles to journey on the path toward righteousness.

Discussion Question

- ▸   What is the importance of intention and struggle in practice?

15.   Divine Guidance of the Sufi and the Mind

There was a Sufi whose life underwent a major change. She was receiving signs that her life would change before it happened. She pondered what was the Divine Guidance behind this change. She thought to herself, "I should continue to follow my mind because I do not know if it is Divine Guidance or a Satanic temptation."

IN PRACTICE

It is important to use the mind as a compass. One should following their reasoning skills but not put too much value on it to avoid being a materialist. In essence, by following the mind, which gives way to reason, and balancing it with the heart, people respect the order and structure that Allah ﷻ established and created. In other words, as some Sufis believe, following the mind is an another way of praying to Allah ﷻ.

Discussion Question

▶ How does one balance the mind and heart?

16. The Angry Divorced Woman and the Sufi

The Sufi encountered an angry woman at work one day. The woman began telling the Sufi her life story. She devoted her entire life to caring for her children and husband. Eventually, her children and husband left her. This is why she was so angry. The Sufi was unhappy and thought to herself, "The best way is to listen and remain silent."

In practice

Sometimes, evil-seeming events can occur in a person's life. In the brief human life span, these are the times and opportunities for self-reflection and self-accountability. Depending on a person's spiritual level, these times may make them more agitated or more committed to the spiritual path. A person who is can become angry when evil-seeming events occur. Or, one can utilize these moments as opportunities for spiritual development. This can make a person stronger, less reliant on other people, and more reliant on Allah ﷻ, who never abandons them and is their true friend.

Discussion Question

- ► How can one use their weak moments as an advantage to spiritually excel?

17.   Life, Power, Evil Beings

The Sufi felt uneasy one day. "There are evil people and unseen evil things," she told herself. "Life is challenging. I am completely powerless." She felt fearful, depressed, and miserable. Then, she began to pray. A few minutes later, she felt strong and confident. She declared, "Alhamdulillah, there is nothing to fear."

IN PRACTICE

It is important to keep daily practices of prayers, litanies, and chants. The cycles of daily rituals can affect the spiritual mode of a spiritual traveler. If a person does not engage in daily worship, prayers, and chants, which is referred to as wird, he or she cannot be immune to temptations, evil thoughts, and evil beings. In the preceding narrative, as soon as the Sufi experienced spiritual contractions and fear, she immediately engaged in prayer.

Discussion Question

- ▶   Why are daily practices of prayers, litanies, and dhikr critical for spiritual soundness?

18. Sufi's Change of Life

One day, the Sufi was contemplating the beauty of prayer, meditation, and Quran reading while she was alone. It gave the Sufi so much pleasure. She did not wish to interact with others. Then, she remembered the teaching of Rasulullah ﷺ regarding being with people and being patient with them, while also maintaining a relationship with Allah ﷻ. The Sufi remarked, "This is so difficult and so painful. I am weary of being harmed. I am exhausted by being around people." But she also recognized that she must be around people in order to maintain a harmonious relationship with Allah ﷻ.

In practice

It is sometimes extremely difficult to interact with others or even be around them These periods of spiritual isolation can last for days, weeks, months, or even years. One is expected to use their mental faculties in accordance with the teachings of Rasulullah ﷺ and the Quran during these times. As in the preceding story, the Sufi's transition was difficult. While her heart remained with Allah ﷻ, she engaged her mind appropriately to implement the change. This was challenging, but achieving this is one of the ideal goals in the practice of one's faith.

Discussion Question

 ▶ How can a person live a balanced social life without harming oneself and others?

19.   Focus, Achievements, and Time

One day, the Sufi was thinking about time. As she drew closer to death, there were still many obstacles in her life that prevented her from achieving her goals. Then, she experienced discomfort, pain, and stress. She questioned, "What should I do?" Then, she prayed to Allah and asked for relief from anxiety, pain, and her fears. Then, she told herself, "I should stick to my plan, do my best, and be consistent on the path until I die."

IN PRACTICE

It is essential to focus on achieving spiritual goals as well as those that benefit others. The essence of prayers chants is to eliminate all distractions from daily discourses and reconnect with the One and Only Allah ﷻ. This focus empowers the individual and can result in spiritual and worldly blessings from Allah ﷻ.

Discussion Question

- ► How can one's unachieved goals be a source of stress? How can one remove this source of stress?

20.   Achievements, Loss, and the Sufi

The Sufi was thinking one day. She was receiving many worldly achievements. She asked herself, "Is this something Allah ☙ approves of, or is it a spiritual plot?"

In practice

Worldly achievements are not signs of spiritual accomplishments. Success, recognition, fame, and power can block one's spiritual goal or purpose. Therefore, it is crucial to maintain doubt and skepticism and ask questions such as the one posed by the Sufi in the story mentioned above.

Discussion Question

▸   How can one define a spiritual achievement?

21. Harvard Shuttle and the Sufi

The Sufi was in Boston one day and noticed a shuttle. There was a banner on the shuttle that read "Harvard loves you." The Sufi contemplated this message. She thought to herself, "Harvard is a university name. People work, teach, and learn there. It is not a human being. How can something abstract love me?"

IN PRACTICE

Abstractions can lead us to assume the existence of life in non-living objects and institutions. It is essential to place everything according to their true purpose and their relationship with Allah. While the statement "Harvard loves you" may be interpreted as a figure of speech, the Sufi is emphasizing that t his saying incorrectly assumes Harvard is an individual who can love, feel, see, and touch. In practice, it is essential to establish the authenticity of meanings in accordance with the Qur'anic definitions and the sayings of the Prophets and Messengers. If not, the individual may be living in a self-created fantasy or dream world, but when confronted with reality, personal devastations or destructions may occur.

Discussion Question

- ▶ What makes illusions seem real?

22.   Difficulty of Being a Real Human

One day, the Sufi pondered the difficulty of being a human. While he knew that he should always be kind, appreciative, and truthful, it was so difficult to put these things into practice. "Alhamdulillah, there is the teaching of Astagfirullah," he thought to himself.

IN PRACTICE

Increasing one's ethical and moral standards through practice is essential. It is also essential to recognize the difficulty of perfecting these as the human body and spirit are constantly changing. It is expected that a strong spiritual connection will increase one's ethics and morality. Even in these circumstances, if there are errors and difficulties, one must ask for forgiveness from people and Allah ﷻ by sincerely chanting "Astagfirullah."

Discussion Question

> ► How can one following ethical and moral standards while balancing the errors and difficulties of life?

23. Worlds of Pens

There was a Sufi who traveled to the world of pens There were numerous pens used for various purposes. Some of the older pens finished their lifespan within a few months. He then met a pen used to write the Qur'an. Many years passed, and the ink remained. The Sufi thought to himself, "I believe the pen is unwilling to die because it enjoys writing the Qur'an."

IN PRACTICE

One may desire a long life in order to do good, enjoy prayers, and read the Qur'an. For a person on life's path, it is important to recognize death is neither ugly nor evil, and it should be preferable to return to the Beloved, Allah ﷻ, and spend eternity with role models, prophets, messengers, and saints.

Discussion Question

 ▶ How do you view dying? Do you prepare yourself mentally and emotionally for the time of death?

24. The Easiness and Difficulty of the True Relationship with One Allah ﷻ

One day, the Sufi pondered the simplicity and difficulty of her relationship with Allah ﷻ. She stated, "It is usually very easy to worship, pray, and make requests only to One Allah ﷻ. However, it becomes difficult to implement these things if I am afraid of others or if praise makes me happy."

In practice

In reality, this is the struggle that must be waged until death in order to elevate one's status with Allah ﷻ, the One and Only Creator. Despite the Quran's assurance that Allah ﷻ is One and Unique, human experience shows that there are difficulties in applying this fundamental concept. In other words, according to the Qur'an, the only acceptable responses to Allah ﷻ are love and reverent fear. The individual should not be pleased when others praise his or her accomplishment. In reality, the individual does not know whether Allah ﷻ is pleased with him or her. Therefore, regular prayers and chants such as la "ilaha illa Allah ﷻ," translated "there is nothing to be attached to other than Allah ﷻ," are essential practices for establishing and perfecting this understanding until death.

Discussion Question

▸   How can one achieve the true level of detachment from everything except Allah ﷻ?

25. Institutional Reality and Changing Identities

The Sufi noticed a course in the college catalog titled "institutional reality." Then, she smiled to herself and stated, "It must teach people how to protect themselves at work by assuming a different identity. I don't think it's worth it."

IN PRACTICE

Changing identities can hurt someone who is going through moments of self-reflection. In an example, changing identities can involve being nice, just, kind, moral, and ethical with one group of people, but not with another, which is problematic. What this can look like in practice is someone appearing to be courteous and kind to their superiors but not to their subordinates. Or, if the individual is pleasant, ethical, and moral at work but not at home. These changing identities can be very harmful during times of solitude and silence, especially when one is nearing death. All the unjust, unkind, immoral, and unethical recollections can torment the individual. Therefore, it is always recommended to live an ethical and moral life without changing identities at work, at home, or on any other occasion during one's brief lifetime. Respect for one's true and genuine self and for Allah ﷻ is essential. If the true and genuine self is dead, a person may still be physically alive, but spiritually lack awareness and morality. Ethical behavior should be embodied as a virtue within oneself.

Discussion Question

- ▶ How can one maintain a genuine self in all of life's endeavors?

26. Justice or Just-Us

There was a Sufi. He had a friend who worked at the court. He told the Sufi: "One day, I was working at the court. A few attorneys were discussing the plaintiff and defendant. The plaintiff had a competent attorney, but the defendant could not afford one. The attorneys were conversing and sarcastically stated, "This defendant does not have an attorney. He will determine whether it is justice or just-us."" The Sufi smiled, but was extremely troubled.

IN PRACTICE

One can remember that there are things we can control and things we cannot control in the face of life's ugliness. Even if one is powerless to stop an injustice or oppressive attitude or action, he or she should still feel disgust for this evil.

Discussion Question

- ▶ How can one abstain from supporting injustices when he or she lacks the ability to affect the situation?

27.   Disciplining for Different Levels

The Sufi was with her son one day. Her son was rambunctious, noisy, and disruptive. The Sufi was attempting to calm her son gently and softly. She feared that others would find her annoying. She remarked to herself, "It's important to gauge everyone's tolerance level. Kids are kids. It's normal for them to have childlike behavior. In contrast, adults are frequently irritated by every noise, sound, and disturbance. This behavior should not be normal."

IN PRACTICE

It is crucial to recognize each individual's tolerance level. If one expects the same things from a person of a different tolerance level, that person may break the individual's future spiritual and physical growth potential.

Discussion Question

- ► How can we take into consideration differences in people's age, gender, and ethnic identities when navigating the world?

28. The Patient and the Sufi

The Sufi visited a friend in the hospital one day. Her friend had cancer and had recently undergone surgery. When the Sufi saw her in the hospital, she was overcome with sorrow and pain. Although the Sufi attempted to comprehend the underlying causes, she still felt pain and distress. She then asked herself, "What can I do to alleviate this discomfort?" She decided to pray at the mosque. She felt better after engaging in prayer.

In practice

There are occurrences in life that disturb us more than others. Always be prepared for "hard-hitting" incidents. If the person regularly engages in worship, prayers, and chants, they can repay the person when disasters strike. In the preceding example, the Sufi had an coping mechanism by going to the mosque, praying, and being alone with Allah ﷻ. If the individual does not know how to navigate these situations, they may be exposed to potentially harmful negative energy.

Discussion Question

> ► How can one develop a spiritual mechanism to cope with evil and good seeming incidents?

29.   Harshness, Teaching, and the Sufi

The Sufi invited a friend to her home one day. Her friend was a nice guy, but she believed in discipline and a bit of harshness in child rearing. The Sufi's children knew the friend. As soon as she arrived, all the children were terrified and well-behaved. The Sufi pondered, "Which is superior? A display of softness that occasionally results in poor treatment by the children, or discipline with a touch of harshness that never results in poor treatment of the children?"

IN PRACTICE

The ideal is to treat everyone, especially children, with kindness, gentleness, and affection. As a role model, Rasulullah ﷺ was the epitome of this quality. Everyone, including women and children, felt at ease around the Prophet. On the other hand, there are some teachers in practice who believe that the concept of discipline or adab should also involve fear in order to prevent disrespectful behavior. Westerners are increasingly critical of the latter approach to discipline in our era of shifting values. But this notion of teaching with discipline should be reconsidered. Historically, discipline and respect were administered differently than they are today.

Discussion Question

- ▶ How do you understand the Eastern and Western cultures in child & parent and student & teacher relationships?

30.   Changing Personalities

The Sufi was working on her project one day. She was pleased that she was able to concentrate, generate new ideas, and complete her daily tasks. She needed to make a few phone calls and send a few emails immediately after completing her work. She felt the need to be in a productive and assertive state. Then, it was nearly three o'clock in the afternoon. She was attempting to change her mental and spiritual state in order to be pleasant and cheerful around her husband and children. Then came the time for prayer and chanting. She began praying. She was contemplating all these methods of personality transformation and their difficulties. Then she thought to herself, "Alhamdulillah, it is possible but not easy."

IN PRACTICE

It is essential to be fully present in different spaces. Due to changing environments, social accidents may sometimes occur. In these situations, the individual may come across as rude, harsh, and uncaring. It is essential to acknowledge the difficulty of altering one's personality while navigating these spaces. Establishing continuous prayers and chants throughout the day is one way to make it simpler. This can aid in concentration, self-reflection, detachment, and the elimination of spiritual toxicity.

Discussion Question

▶   Can a person assume only one personality? Why or why not?

31. Internal World, External World, and the Difficulties of Interaction

One day, the Sufi was reflecting on the wonders of the internal world: silence, reflection, thought, and solitude. She was in great pleasure. Then she began to consider the ugliness of the external world: talking, marketing, socializing, and pretending. She was so disgusted. "How do I make the transition from one to the other?" she wondered. "It's always so painful."

In practice

This is the real struggle. Being involved with external affairs while being with Allah ﷻ through prayers, reading, chanting, reflection, and thought. It can seem like these two worlds are diametrically opposed. However As a result, a person can live in the present moment for the sake of bettering his or her future. In other words, the person can interact with people for Allah ﷻ's sake so that when the person meets Allah ﷻ after death, he or she can sincerely state that this person was in the world for Allah's ﷻ pleasure. Ultimately, Allah ﷻ has the power to reward this person for his or her genuine efforts in the world.

Discussion Question

- ▶ How can one solace oneself about the unknowns of future by making an intention of living their life in order to please Allah ﷻ?

32.   Cancer, Funeral, and the Sufi

There was once someone who smoked. The Sufi recognized him. He became ill and was diagnosed with lung cancer. The doctors informed the family that he would die soon due to advanced cancer. The Sufi went to see the person, said some prayers, and tried to console the family. When the Sufi returned home, he told his children about his visit and talked about the brevity of life, the value of time, and the frailty of humans. A few days later, the Sufi learned that the man had died. The Sufi's children were also informed of the tragic news. Everyone was impacted.

IN PRACTICE

Death is an unavoidable reality. People are expected to take a thoughtful approach to preparing for death. Although physical means of preparation such as wills, funeral arrangements, or letters to loved ones are important, the real preparation is meeting with Allah ﷻ. Sometimes Allah ﷻ sends tribulations, sicknesses, or difficulties as the final performance of a person's life journey in order to elevate the person's status before meeting with Allah ﷻ. Although people may experience distress in evil-seeming incidents, it is, as Rumi says, "like a wedding day for those who are longing and preparing to meet with Allah ﷻ."

Discussion Question

▶   How can a person make preparations for their death?

33.   The Clear and the Mystical Teachings

One day, the Sufi considered starting a business. She had all the indications that she should begin immediately. She then realized it was a Tuesday, not a Wednesday. Then she considered whether she should follow the mystical signs that said she should begin the venture on Tuesday. Or if she should follow the obvious signs and begin on Wednesday. "If there are clear ones, those are preferred over the mystical ones," she said. She then decided to launch her new business on Wednesday.

IN PRACTICE

When the heart and mind disagree, it is critical to listen to the mind. In other words, if there are clear teachings and guidelines through scripture and the Prophet's practice, the person is expected to follow the clear ones over the mystical ones. If there are no clear ones, or if there is room for interpretation due to a lack of clear ones, then mystical signs can be useful. In the preceding story, there is a tradition that Rasulullah ﷺ used to start new things on Wednesdays [10]. As a result, the Sufi chose that path over mystical signs.

Discussion Question

▶ How do you understand the concept of contradiction between heart and mind?

34. Little Minds Thinking Big

The Sufi took her four-year-old to a science museum one day. There were dinosaur skeletons and other fossils. Her four-year-old son was fascinated and kept asking questions. The Sufi was taken aback by the caliber of the questions from a four-year-old. She thought to herself, "Wow, a person can begin the journey at the age of four. The important part is determining how to help them on this path of learning and growing."

IN PRACTICE

It is critical to recognize that small minds can think big. If they are not engaged correctly in this process of imagination, these memories and conversations can come back to the person after years of childhood and adulthood. Personal religious experience can begin as early as childhood with an understanding of nature, art, and sounds. On the other hand, some Sufi scholars try to limit their children's exposure to visual and auditory media such as pictures or music. Their reasoning is that a child may not understand how to translate meanings from visual and auditory sources into meanings. As a result, in their pursuit of a positive relationship with the Divine, these visual and auditory media can become isolating.

Discussion Question

> ► How do you relate your childhood religious experience to your current religious practice?

35.   Anger, Difficulty, and the Sufi

A month passed. The Sufi was extremely kind to her children. One day, the children did something annoying and disrespectful to their mother. She screamed angrily at them. She finally calmed down after a while. "I was doing fine for so long and didn't get angry" she told herself. "What happened to me?" She returned to her children and explained why she was angry, gave them advice, and asked for forgiveness.

IN PRACTICE

Giving advice is valuable. The manner in which the advice is given may be more important than the content of the advice. In other words, it is extremely difficult to give advice without becoming angry while also conveying the message in such a way that others are not offended. This communication and attitude can be more difficult to maintain with people we see every day at work or at home. It is also necessary to be sorry for how we speak or feel about others. It is a virtue to express regret and seek forgiveness from others when one has caused harm.

Discussion Question

► Do you practice self-reflection often?

36. Spiritual Hunting with Distractions

The Sufi was working on spiritual searching one day. In other words, she was praying, chanting, and reading the Qurān and the hadith. She was attempting to reflect, comprehend, draw, and contextualize these meanings. She referred to this as "spiritual hunting." She had forgotten to turn off her phone. When she heard text messages from her phone while deep in meditation, she told herself, "If I look at the screen, I will lose all the focus that I have built up." So she ignored them. Nonetheless, she wondered if it was an emergency. She then checked her phone after she was finished. It wasn't anything significant, she said, "Alhamdulillah, thanks to Allah ﷻ."

IN PRACTICE

It is critical to fully engage and focus during spiritual discharge and charge moments. One should be able to disconnect from their surroundings. Most spiritual advancements come, appear, and are given by Allah ﷻ during those moments of concentration. These are possibly the last days. However, these spiritual engagements require warm-up, peak, and cool-down periods. It's very similar to physical activity. Although the Sufi in the preceding story had responsibilities to others, she continued in her engagement and after she was finished took proper action in the case of an emergency.

Discussion Question

- ▶ How do you interpret the phrase "spiritual hunting"?

37. Life, Desires, Pleasures, and Death

The Sufi was thinking about life and desires one day. She desired to enjoy personal pleasures, such as eating or having fun. However, every time she attempted these things, she was reminded of death, and she was unable to enjoy herself. "What should I do?" she wondered. She thought about it for a while and decided the best action was to pray. After praying, she was feeling a lot better. Then, she began eating a delicious meal while her mind and heart were engaged with Allah ﷻ. She exclaimed, "Wow, I am enjoying this meal! Perhaps this is the key."

In practice

One can transform worldly pleasure into infinite pleasure by staying in relationship with Allah ﷻ. In other words, if someone enjoys something solely for the sake of its pleasure, the end result may be painful for that person. However, if one knows how to connect immediate pleasures of the world to spiritual pleasures, then the person can fully benefit from them. In other words, when a person appreciates all the pleasures of the world in their relationship with Allah ﷻ, the person knows that Allah ﷻ will give more in the world and after death as a result.

Discussion Question

- Do you find that thinking about death makes you enjoy life's pleasures? Why or why not?

38. Nights and Sleep

The Sufi was thinking about his sleep one day. "I'm sleeping so much at night, 11 p.m.–6:30 a.m.," he told himself. It is a waste of time, even though I get up early in the morning, perform, and enjoy my work. "What should I do?" he asked himself.

In practice

Sleeping is beneficial as long as it is done in moderation. Similar to eating, a person can make intentions to sleep so that he or she will be refreshed to worship and grow closer to Allah ﷻ. On the other hand, because nights are special in one's relationship with Allah ﷻ, there is an encouragement to use a portion of the night for prayers and worship. Most should follow the Prophetic advice of waking up in the last third of the night, a few hours before sunrise, and engaging in sincere, genuine, and solitary worship of the Divine.

39.   People, Disappointments, and Dilemma

Every time the Sufi socialized with others, she regretted it. "I don't know why I came here," she used to say. "I told myself that staying by myself, worshipping, chanting, and reading the scripture is far preferable to being subjected to social gatherings." The Sufi was once again disappointed. She was also torn between solitude and service to others through socializing.

IN PRACTICE

Solitude can be enjoyable when combined with worship, chanting, and reading the Quran, all of which help to expand one's mindful and spiritual knowledge and experience. When interacting with others, a spiritually active Sufi should constantly monitor one's inner feelings and thoughts, as they may intensify. An as analogy, an active person can have rapid blood flow. If the exercise is not done as recommended by fitness trainers, the person may suffer a heart attack and die. Similarly, when a person is with others, if feelings and thoughts such as arrogance, vanity, jealousy arise, they should be caught and removed with "astagfirullah" according to the methods suggested by spiritual trainers.

40. Cats, Dogs, and the Sufi

There was a Sufi who traveled to Turkey to see a friend. As she walked the streets of Istanbul, s he was surprised to see wandering cats and dogs without leashes and their owners. She then asked her friend, "Can these dogs be dangerous without leashes or owners?" "They are just living with us," her Sufi friend explained, "they are a part of our daily lives."

IN PRACTICE

There are many Sufi stories about cats and dogs. Barking dogs during the call to prayer is a common occurrence in Muslim countries. According to the traditional interpretation, dogs bark because they see Satan running. There are numerous cat stories about visiting mosques. Rasulullah ﷺ bestowed the title of "father of cats" on one of his close friends, "Abu Huraira." Abu Huraira adored and spent a lot of time with the cats. Abu Huraira spent the majority of his time with Rasulullah ﷺ, learning from him. As a result, Abu Huraira recorded and transmitted many of the narrations and practices[3] about Rasulullah ﷺ's life.

---

3. Hadith.

41. Fame, Allah ﷻ's Pleasure ,and the Sufi

One day, the Sufi was thinking about fame, public recognition, and recognition by Allah ﷻ. She examined her heart and ego. Her ego craved fame and recognition. At the same time, her heart desired Allah ﷻ's recognition. The Sufi then thought to herself, "How might the two go together?" She pondered this dilemma but was unable to resolve it.

IN PRACTICE

Fame can be a poison on the spiritual path of developing a genuine relationship with Allah ﷻ. If Allah ﷻ is pleased and happy with this person, he or she has the potential to become famous. Still, fame can separate a person from Allah ﷻ if the person does not understand the purpose of what he or she is doing. On the other hand, there are many secret saints known and loved only by Allah ﷻ. In this case, the person is less vulnerable to the poisonous strikes of fame and people. In this regard, the person on the path should dislike receiving compliments from others.

42.   Trials, Position of the Heart, and Detachment

One day, the Sufi was contemplating the wisdom behind trials, tribulations, and difficulties. Then she met a friend who had a very wealthy and nice life but was unattached to her possessions. She later met another friend who was poor, sick, and constantly afraid of becoming even poorer and losing what she had. The Sufi then looked at the two cases and thought to herself, "I found the wisdom. You must detach from your possessions in order to enjoy life."

IN PRACTICE

A person's life can be easy or difficult, rich or poor. It makes no difference. The position of the heart is important because it changes whether or not a person is attached to his or her belongings. If a person's heart is the same in the happiest and the most difficult times of his or her life, then that person is detached from everything except Allah ﷻ. This is known as zuhd. It becomes a spiritual state when it becomes a person's constant trait. This person will then experience true joy, happiness, and heaven.

43.   Heaven 1, Heaven 2, and the Sufi

The Sufi was constantly thankful and grateful to Allah ﷻ. She was always cheerful, whether things were going well or not. "I am already having my first Heaven in the world," she thought to herself. "I hope to be in the second Heaven after death."

In practice

There is a state of consistent gratitude, or station.[i] When a person reaches this state, both sadness and happiness become equal. Some people may only experience temporary gratitude. For others, this state may be permanent. This is referred to as station.

44. Cat Hanging around with Humans and the Sufi

There was a cat who liked to hang out with people. She disliked being around other cats because she found them annoying. This cat thought humans were perfect and wished she could be like them. When someone entered the house, she would approach them and hug them. The Sufi recognized the situation and told the cat, "Being a human is not as easy as you think."

IN PRACTICE

One of humankinds' faults is the desire to be like others rather than being ourselves. Allah ﷻ has blessed us abundantly. Gratitude and appreciation increase the bounty. According to the Quran[ii], if a person thanks and appreciates all of life's bounties, Allah ﷻ will increase them even more. In the preceding story, the Sufi felt his cat was in the same situation. He tried to convince her that humans, with their flaws and imperfections, are not perfect.

45. Quotidian Refreshing Rituals, Exceptions, and the Sufi

The Sufi planned to travel one day. She considered missing her daily prayers, chants, and meditation with Allah ﷻ. This ritual practice was critical to the Sufi. She was very worried about this. She then began her journey. She was able to find a corner to establish her spiritual space and continue her regular spiritual habits while on the plane, in the airport, and on the train. She finished it and said, "Alhamdulillah, thank you Allah ﷻ, You gave me the ability to be attached to You even while traveling."

In practice

The importance of daily prayers, chants, and meditations cannot be overstated. In practice, this is known as Wird or Awrad. "If there is no wird, there is no spiritual refreshment and spiritual discoveries,"[iii] as the saying goes. From this vantage point, a person's day has meaning through his or her discoveries and spiritual quests. If a day goes by without this, it can be considered a wasted day.

46.   Patience, Difficulty, and the Sufi

The Sufi was traveling with her family one day. It had been a long journey to another country. The journey was extremely exhausting. The children were sobbing. It was extremely difficult to use the restroom. "I am not going to travel again," the husband complained. It's extremely difficult." The Sufi inhaled deeply and continued chanting and praying to Allah ﷻ for ease.

IN PRACTICE

As the Prophet[6]iv mentioned, traveling can be a form of torture from hell. Patience is defined as not acting negatively in difficult situations. Engaging in prayer and chanting, as mentioned in the Quran, is one way to practice patience. Complaining does not help and may make the situation worse.

47.   Heart Diseases, Detection, and the Sufi

The Sufi was praying in a park one day. Her children were having fun. Another family and a young girl were present. The Sufi gave each of her children one candy. When her children asked for seconds, she said "no." Then a small girl approached the Sufi and requested candy. The Sufi gave her a piece of candy. Then, when the girl had finished her candy, she came over and asked for another. "What should I say?" pondered the Sufi. I still have a few candies left. They are pricey." The Sufi instructed the young girl to wait. The Sufi was looking through her bag to see if she could give the small girl anything else. When the small girl's mother realized this, she became enraged at her daughter. The Sufi was horrified and exclaimed, "My stinginess!"

In practice

In the preceding story, the Sufi immediately attempted to detect her spiritual disease in the incident rather than blaming the mother. It is important to be aware of one's own spiritual diseases. Stinginess is a disease that can be difficult to detect at times. It is a sign of attachment, which is the negative spiritual state.[v] However, by recognizing one's spiritual disease, one can turn it around into a positive spiritual state.

Discussion Question

> ▸   Is it difficult to detect one's own spiritual diseases? Why?

48.   Easiness in Practice, and the Effect of the Place

The Sufi went to a very spiritual place, the holy sites, one day.[vi] Everybody was praying. In comparison to other places, he found praying and all spiritual activities to be very easy. Then he thought to himself, "Wow, it must be the place's effect!"

IN PRACTICE

Positive spiritual locations have angelic and spiritual beings that can make the spiritual world very easy to engage with. For millions of people praying together 24 hours a day for hundreds of years, holy sites are the ultimate spiritual places. The gathering of positive angelic and spiritual beings can make this location natural for positive spiritual experiences. On the other hand, places of evil and bad engagements can cause a person to engage in ill thoughts, depression, and even evil action.

49.   The Children as Blessing but Not as a Trial

The Sufi awoke one day to the sound of children screaming. "Again, the same, dealing with their screaming and giving me a hard time before they go to school," she told herself. Then she remembered the teachings in the Quran and from Rasulullah ﷺ about children, that they can be both a trial and a blessing. Then she told herself, "I hope they become a blessing for me rather than a trial."

IN PRACTICE

It is critical to understand that every engagement, affiliation, or accumulation can be a blessing or a curse. Wealth, children, position, beauty, or health, as well as spiritual commitments, can be blessings, trials, or tests. As a result, it is always necessary to ask Allah ﷻ to transform all evil-seeming and good-seeming engagements, affiliations, and accumulations into true blessings in this life and the afterlife.

50. The Physicist Sufi, Superconductors at Zero, and the Self

A Sufi was contemplating the law of superconductors at absolute zero. At this temperature, there is no friction. He stated that when one is at absolute zero, humble, one can go beyond the friction of the ego and self.[4] Then there's the superconducting and joyful person in this world and the afterlife. There is not friction of the nafs.[5]

In practice

There are various levels of self. The raw self is the initial self.[vii] This type of self is always running behind his or her desires. In other words, the desires of this self have the ability to command the person. As a person attends various spiritual trainings, he or she may begin to disregard the orders of the self. The person can act in accordance with the mind, heart, Scripture, and Prophet. One of the higher stages of the self is present on this journey. At this point, the person achieves complete spiritual freedom from the prison of the evil self.[viii] This could be analogous to the superconducting case in spiritual physics in the preceding story.

---

4. Nafs.
5. Raw Self or ego acting towards evil with spiritual sickness.

51. The Sufi with Bald Head and Long Hair

A Sufi was contemplating the impact of spirituality on both long and shaved hair. He thought to himself, "In both cases, the effects are vastly different." Long hair heightens softness and spiritual inspiration. Shaved hair promotes more justice and mindfulness. A Sufi can exist in both worlds.

IN PRACTICE

The individual should be in a balanced state of mind and heart. Rasulullahﷺ wore his hair long at times and shaved at others. According to the Quran, shaving and shortening one's hair after a pilgrimage can provide security and alleviate fears. Rasulullah ﷺ and many of his companions, on the other hand, had long hair.[5] Rasulullah ﷺ also spoke about Jesus' curly hair.[6] [5]

52.   The Sufi and the Kufi

The Sufi wore his hair long. He placed the Kufi, or head cover, on his head. He was slipping and falling every time he put on the Kufi. The Sufi was sick of it. He then decided to shave his head and don the Kufi. He had his hair shaved. When he put on the Kufi, it became firmly attached to his head. When the Sufi tried to remove the Kufi, it was difficult because the sharp shaved hair held the Kufi in place. The Sufi grew tired of it as well.

In practice

It is critical to strike a balance between the heart and the mind. Long hair, according to some mystics, represents spirituality,[11] the heart, and complete detachment. The bald or shaved head, on the other hand, can represent the realms of the mind, reasons, and following causality. In practice, an ideal person is expected to have both states. Rasulullah ﷺ had both long hair and a shaved head.[6] [5] [9] [12]

53. The Life, the Kids, and the Trials

The Sufi had a disagreement with her daughter one day. Her daughter was in her adolescence and pretended to know everything. The daughter refused to interact with her parents in public. The Sufi mother was becoming increasingly irritated by her daughter's attitude. "What should I do?" she pondered, "I should act rationally, but I can't." She went to pray for guidance in solitude.

In practice

It is critical to anticipate potential issues with age, culture, gender, and kinship relationships. The Sufis strive to act wisely in order to reduce the number of times when one can say, "I wish I hadn't done that." Although it is difficult to maintain peace of mind when dealing with children's issues and attitudes, it is still expected to act with wisdom, patience, and counsel.

54. Optimizing the Time before Death

One day, the Sufi reflected on the cycles of sleep, chats, eating, and engagements that do not result in immediate spiritual output. "How can I optimize my time?" he asked herself. He then reduced his sleep, chitter-chatter, and food intake. He was happy. "This should be the key," he said.

IN PRACTICE

For sleeping, talking, and eating, it is a general rule to not overindulge. A person who succeeds in decreasing these three, in a healthy way, can progress steadily in their spiritual journey.[13]

55. Departure, Crying, and the Sufi

There was once a Sufi who refused to visit the holy sites. His friends used to go to the holy sites every year, but he never did. When asked why, he explained, "I don't want to cry when I leave the holy places."

In practice

Spiritual attachments can also be painful. This pain has the potential to be both powerful and positive. The agony of seeing the Beloved and missing Allah ﷻ is a noble and high level of agony. Allah ﷻ appreciates this suffering in ways that humans cannot comprehend.

56. Poverty, Happiness, and Connection

The Sufi paid a visit to a poor neighborhood in Cairo one day. Despite their poverty, she discovered that everyone was content. She visited their mosque. Everyone was praying, chatting, and smiling. "That must be the reason," she reasoned to herself.

IN PRACTICE

Religion is essential for achieving happiness in one's life. External well-being does not bring lasting peace to the heart, though it can have immediate and temporary effects. Genuine religious prayers can lead to a heavenly life in the world, while others may feel bad about them due to a lack of social and economic conditions.

57.   The Sufi Having Egyptian Coffee

The Sufi was in a Cairo coffee shop one day. In Egypt, the Sufi enjoyed various types of coffee. He was chatting with the store owner while drinking coffee. According to the owner, the elite Egyptians prefer Starbucks to local coffee. "I don't know why people always want what they don't have," the Sufi said.

IN PRACTICE

The first step toward gratitude and thankfulness to Allah ﷻ is to have a positive attitude toward what one has. In this sense, support for local businesses is analogous to someone appreciating what he or she has on the spiritual journey.

58.   Thirsty Child and the Sufi

The Sufi was in the car with her child one day. Her child became thirsty. "Can I have some water?" he asked his mother. "OK," his mother said, "we'll get a bottle for you when we stop at a gas station." The child was extremely thirsty. He kept asking every minute or so. "OK, I'll get it soon," his mother kept saying. "Sorry, I forgot to ask before," the child said. A minute later, the child asked the same question. "I should stop immediately," the mother told herself, "or he'll keep asking."

In practice

When a person is thirsty, the need to find water becomes extremely pressing. This desire may cause the person to seek water as soon as possible. Similarly, if the individual is not on a spiritual path, he or she cannot benefit from the overflowing wisdom from meditation, prayers, and retreats.

59. Checking the Heart

The Sufi went to a poor neighborhood in Cairo one day. The Sufi was staying in a luxurious, pricey hotel. She went for a walk outside. There were many beggars who came to the Sufi and asked for money. The Sufi tried to keep some money for the poor in her pocket at all times. While she was giving the money to one beggar, other beggars approached her and requested more money from the Sufi. The Sufi stated that her money had been spent. The beggar was adamant. The Sufi was unsettled. For a moment, the Sufi reflected on her heart to see if she had any judgment feelings toward the beggar. "Alhamdulillah, but it was not easy," she said.

IN PRACTICE

It is important to constantly monitor one's heart. All types of arrogance, judging others, feelings of superiority, disgust, and ridicule are examples of heart-threatening behaviors. In the preceding example, the Sufi attempted to assist people without judging them and with compassion for their circumstances. In the case of one beggar insisting on more money, she attempted to neutralize any negative feelings she may have had towards the beggar. Although the Sufi stayed in an expensive hotel, the true state of the heart can be revealed by detachment from worldly pursuits. It is not the physical or external detachment, but the heart's detachment from everything other than Allah ﷻ.

Discussion Question

- ▶ How one can make the habit of checking their hearts? Is this difficult?

60.   Funeral, Crying, and the Sufi

One day, the Sufi arrived at his residence. He heard his wife crying and talking on the phone in the same room. As soon as the Sufi heard the word "funeral," he grasped the situation. Without entering the room, the Sufi sat and engaged in his daily rituals of meditation and prayer. Then, his wife exited the room and informed him of their loss. Sufi remarked, "We belong to Allah ﷻ and will return back to Allah ﷻ."

In practice

A daily routine of meditation, prayer, and reflection time is essential. This becomes more important when a person is confronted with an evil-seeming event. This routine practice enables the individual to maintain spiritual composure during these times. Instead of immediately telling his wife about the loss, the Sufi prayed to Allah ﷻ for the spiritual fortitude to assist others. After gaining strength from his daily routine of meditation, prayer, and reflection, he assisted his wife.

61.   The Best Place in Town: Graveyard

One day, the Sufi visited a family member in a Cairo town. The city was overrun with people, buildings, and automobiles. The streets were dirty. Cars were constantly beeping. A few days later, the Sufi learned that a family member had passed away. He then attended the funeral and traveled to the cemetery for the burial. The cemetery was so beautiful. It contained olive trees. The Sufi felt extremely tranquil and peaceful there. Then he thought to himself, "This is the best spot in town."

IN PRACTICE

The graveyards are inhabited by individuals who can hear but cannot speak. The tranquility of the cemetery may be attributable to the deceased's high spiritual standing with Allah ﷻ. In Madina, it is recommended to visit the grave of Rasulullah ﷺ. Visitors anonymously report that the atmosphere surrounding the Prophet's tomb is serene. In contrast, if there is a grave of a wicked person, it is advised not to linger around it but to quickly pass it by. It is advised to plant trees on gravesites. As trees are living creatures, they pray, chant, and praise Allah ﷻ. When the deceased hears chants, prayers, and glorifications of Allah ﷻ in the grave, he or she feels better.[14][15] Therefore, it is also advised that, when visiting a grave, one reads scripture and prays.

62. Heart, Changes, and Level

The Sufi visited her hometown one day. She saw her friends and family. She visited the locations where she once hung out. All memories were so pleasant. The time had come to depart. The Sufi experienced some unease in her heart. Then, she reflected, "my low level." Then, she engaged in prayer, scripture reading, and chanting until the unease in her heart subsided. She said "Alhamdulillah."

IN PRACTICE

It is important not to attach one's heart to anything. If there are traces of attachment, such as feelings of uneasiness or sadness, as in the preceding example, one can engage in prayers, recitations of the Qur'an, and chants until these emotions disappear. In practice, the only way to live a truly happy life is to completely detach and release one's heart from everything other than Allah ﷻ.

63. Nights and Purpose

The Sufi awoke in the middle of the night one day to pray to Allah ﷻ. The only person awake in the house was the Sufi. She began praying in seclusion. She reflected on her past life, recalling where and with whom she had spent time. She contemplated the remainder of her life and how and where she should devote her efforts. She then reaffirmed her intent and stated, "I began this journey to please Allah ﷻ, and I should conclude it in the same way."

IN PRACTICE

It is essential to complete the journey with the same good and noble intentions with which it was begun. There are many people who begin their lives with good intentions but abandon them as their lives progress. Along the journey, constant self-reflection to diagnose one's intention, position, and purpose is essential. Nighttime is crucial for this purpose. The individual can pray, cry, and engage in self-reflection when he or she awakens after a restful night's sleep, while others are still asleep. Rasulullah ﷺ prayed at night while everyone else was asleep.[6]ix Therefore, many of Allah ﷻ's devotees excel at nighttime spiritual journeys.

Discussion Question

▶ Why is it important to check one's intentions before taking action?

64. Chats Leading to Disturbance

The Sufi was conversing with his mother one day. As the Sufi did not like to speak excessively so as not to make mistakes and displease Allah, he thought to himself, "This is my elderly mother; allow me to converse briefly to amuse her. The Sufi began conversing in a manner similar to that of others. Discussing the weather, food, children, and people. As the conversation turned to people, the Sufi became slightly uneasy. He attempted not to backbite or speak ill of others. As the conversation continued, the Sufi said something about a person that upset him so much, and he thought to himself, "I wish I had kept my usual silence."

IN PRACTICE

Prophetic encouragements include maintaining silence, smiling, and extending greetings.[5][6] One is expected to have a reason for speaking if they do so. Sins such as backbiting, displaying signs of arrogance, etc., can cause unease in the heart, which can be triggered by aimless chatter or conversations. It is extremely difficult to achieve a balance between the two modes of social life compared to one's life as an introvert. Rasulullah ﷺ was an excellent example of this balance. He used to always greet people with a smile. Everyone felt very at ease around him. On the other hand, his speech was purposeful. His speech was extremely concise, to the point, and dense with multiple meanings. There are numerous narrations in which the number of words he used while speaking could have been easily counted[6].

65. Balance between Solitude and Social Life

A Sufi felt incredibly alone on her spiritual journey one day. She typically enjoyed solitude, as well as the responsibility of instructing and learning from others. Then, she became uneasy. She asked herself, "What ought I to do? Having students sometimes brings arrogance. Learning from others in social settings always carries the potential for spiritual chaos." Then, she said, "I must do it if Rasulullah ﷺ did and suggested it."

In practice

There are some who are not concerned with having students, but rather their close relationship with Allah ﷻ. Although these individuals exist, they may be uncommon and are certainly not universal. As a general rule, it is essential to give back to our fellow humans through teaching and other forms of service. As the Sufi mentioned, teaching can occasionally attract the unwelcome guests of haughtiness and a negative reputation due to the followers or students. However, the individual is expected to exercise self-responsibility in order to eliminate these diseases. Because all good comes from Allah ﷻ and all evil-seeming events are the result of human endeavors. On the other hand, the Sufi mentioned the issue of spiritual disorder in social learning encounters. One should cultivate the ability to balance and transform oneself from spiritual chaos to spiritual clarity. This may not be simple, but it is the essence of spiritual struggle throughout one's lifetime.

Discussion Question

- How can one make a balance between social life and solitude?

66. Life, Responsibilities, and Balance

The Sufi contemplated her obligations to her children, family, friends, and other humans one day. Then, she thought to herself, I must uphold and maintain these obligations to please Allah ﷻ. It is extremely difficult to strike this balance without breaking hearts while fulfilling these responsibilities.

IN PRACTICE

The transition between secular and spiritual matters can be challenging. There is a level at which a person can live among worldly people while his or her mind, heart, and spirit are with Allah ﷻ. This is the ideal objective to attain. Prophets exemplify this practice. Even in various passages of the Qur'an, those who challenge the prophets raise the question of how someone who eats and drinks like us can claim to be a messenger of Allah ﷻ. This person serves as a model for all spiritual matters. In His infinite wisdom, Allah ﷻ sends us these messengers and prophets as examples of how difficult it is to be with Allah ﷻ while living among people. This is the desired outcome, and it is achievable.

## 67.	Darkness and Belief

The Sufi felt uneasy about his life one day. As soon as he engaged in prayers, Quran reading, and chanting, he felt better. When he ended this engagement, he once again felt a great deal of spiritual darkness and distress. He asked himself, "What is the answer?" Then he thought to himself, "The challenge is to be with Allah ﷻ while engaging in worldly affairs among people."

IN PRACTICE

The heart of a person who is engaged in the remembrance of Allah ﷻ in any form, including prayers, reading the Qur'an, litanies, and divine chants, is refreshed and made tranquil. This is stated in the Qur'an: "Only the remembrance of Allah ﷻ can calm the hearts."[x] It can be difficult to reconcile times of peace and tranquility with the heart's fluctuating states of distress and contraction. In times of darkness and distress, it is advised that the individual immediately return to their regular rituals, such as prayers, readings, litanies, and chants.

68.   Out of Trouble Man and Marriage in Heaven

The Sufi used to be acquainted with a poor wise-fool. Each time the Sufi encountered this man, he would say, "Alhamdulillah, praise be to Allah ﷻ, I am free of trouble." The Sufi formerly referred to him as "out of trouble man." The Sufi attended a funeral one day. He saw the trouble-free man at the funeral and gave him a ride afterward. During their conversation in the car, the Sufi asked him, "Are you married?" He replied, "No, I am not married now, but I will be in Heaven, inshAllah." I am eagerly anticipating it." The Sufi exclaimed, "What a spiritual level to be at!"

In practice

It is recommended to marry. As always, there are exceptional cases to general rules. There are individuals who may not be married because they devote their lives to studying, praying, and teaching. They may believe that if they marry, they will not be able to fulfill the responsibilities of a spouse. As in the preceding story, there are a great number of wise people who may have a high spiritual level with Allah ﷻ and who may sometimes conceal their identity by acting foolish. They are known as wise fools. The wise-fool in the preceding story did not marry during his lifetime and may have devoted his life to worship and solitude with the intention of marrying in Heaven after his death.

69. Anger, Ugliness, and the Mirror

One day, the Sufi became enraged with his children. Previously, he would immediately rush to the mirror to examine his face. Again, he went to examine his face. It looked so horrible. He continued to look until he calmed down. He said: "a'uzubillahi min ashaytani rajim," (I take refuge in Allah-God from the damned Satan." He felt better. His anger had subsided.

In practice

One of the negative spiritual states is rage. There are times when anger is commendable, but they are rare and not the norm. When a person is angry, all of his or her spiritual states are destroyed. In the preceding story, the Sufi observed his face's ugliness in order to use it as a means of relaxation. As anger is attributed to Satan, one's face can reflect these ugly and satanic expressions in these negative states. In order to avoid succumbing to Satan's temptations, "a'uzubillahi min ashaytani rajim" is one of the Prophetic sayings against anger.

70.   Allah ﷻ, Humans, and Measure Stick

One day, the Sufi became enraged with his children. Even though he had advised them repeatedly, they did not pay attention. When they were infants, he was responsible for changing their diapers, carrying them on his shoulder, and feeding them. He felt his children no longer valued him as a parent. Then he thought to himself, "Allah ﷻ has no children. We are all products of nothing. The Creator has more rights over creation than parents do over their children. I now comprehend how Allah ﷻ can be so Patient, Forgiving, and Forbearing in comparison to us, as parents."

In practice

It is essential to remember that Allah creates everything with intention, purpose, and wisdom. The relationship between children and their parents can serve as a barometer for one's relationship with Allah ﷻ. Allah ﷻ recommends in the Qur'an respect, kindness, and gentleness toward one's parents. When a person develops a sense of gratitude and appreciation for others, particularly those to whom they owe a great debt, he or she naturally develops an appreciative relationship with Allah ﷻ. Rasulullah ﷺ mentions that a person who does not thank others for their favors is incapable of thanking Allah ﷻ[12].

71.   Different Names of Allah ☙ and Daily Affairs

One day, the Sufi and her son were traveling. They were on the aircraft. The aircraft took off. Her son stated, "Mom, I have to go potty; I can't hold it any longer." All seatbelt signs were illuminated, and no one was permitted to get up. The Sufi instructed her son to recite the Name of Allah ☙, Al-Qabid. The kid starting saying it. After a few moments, the boy stated, "I no longer need to use the restroom." The mom said, "Alhamdulillah."

IN PRACTICE

Allah has a variety of names and attributes. By studying these Divine Names, one can approximate the proper understanding of Allah ☙. As in the preceding story, there is a recommendation to memorize and recite these names frequently in various life situations. The Sufi understood that one of Allah ☙'s Names is Al-Qabid, the Contractor or the Holder. In this hopeless circumstance, she instructed her son to recite this Name. The urge of the boy was then restrained by reciting this Name of Allah ☙. A person can be prescribed the appropriate number of repetitions of various Names of Allah ☙ in various situations, similar to a prescription medication.

72. Hugging, Anger, and Child

The Sufi became angry with his children one day. The youngest son approached his father and began to embrace and kiss him. He then began kissing and hugging him as well. The Sufi then said to himself, "I was enraged, but no longer. "What happened to me?"

IN PRACTICE

It is essential to be insistent and demanding when asking Allah ﷻ for forgiveness. When a person prays and asks Allah ﷻ for forgiveness, Rasulullah ﷺ instructs that he or she should be firm and insistent.[1]xi Allah ﷻ can do anything. In practice, there is no human association of anger with Allah ﷻ. Anger is a negative trait and a flaw in human discourse.

73. Controlling the Heart and Thoughts

One day, the Sufi encountered a person who was critical of others' flaws and disrespectful in religious matters. One year later, the Sufi was invited to a social event. The Sufi was uncertain as to whether he should leave. He did not have a distinct purpose for attending the gathering. Then, he decided to attend and ran into the same rude and disrespectful individual at this social event. The individual was paralyzed. The Sufi felt sorry for him and attempted to stop his thoughts and heart's disposition regarding the potential causes of this person's difficulty.

In practice

It is crucial to have a reason for doing or not doing something. A person's relationship with Allah ﷻ may be jeopardized if he or she has merely the intention of having fun, or no intention at all. In the preceding story, when the Sufi attended the gathering and saw the person who used to be rude and disrespectful, he felt an immediate urge to connect what had happened to him to his previous improper attitude toward people and religion. Now, the Sufi placed himself in a difficult position of self-control as he fought against and prevented these thoughts from entering his mind and heart. In actuality, one does not judge others based on their difficulties. There are numerous instances in which people who pass judgment on others experience the same problems and issues.

74. Cheap Paper Cup and the Sufi

The Sufi was drinking coffee one day. She used to consume coffee from a paper cup and reuse the cup. She consumed coffee one day and then washed the cup the following day. She spent a great deal of time cleaning it for a fresh cup of coffee. Immediately after she poured the coffee, there were some drips. The Sufi examined the cup and remarked, "It probably leaked while I was drinking." Then, she carefully took another sip, but there was another drip. She thought to herself, "I need to be more careful about where my lips touch the cup." The third time she took a sip with extreme caution, there was another drip. Then, she inspected the cup's base. She recognized the leak and remarked, "What a cheap paper cup!"

IN PRACTICE

Occasionally, a person places a high value on an unauthentic practice or teaching. A person may devote years to following or engaging in a practice with high hopes, but without understanding its true value. A bad disappointment can result from squandering one's efforts after a lengthy period of time. Consequently, it is essential to assign the correct value to everything. A genuine teaching, a trustworthy teacher, or a genuine practice will not disappoint the individual in this life or the next.

75. Self-Control, Willpower, and Environment

One day, the Sufi intended to spend time with his children and family at home. He told himself, "No matter what the children do, I will not be angry." Indeed, he once again lost himself and became angry. He hurried to the mosque immediately for prayer, meditation, and Quran reading. Immediately following an hour of prayer, he felt his true, calm, and peaceful self. Then, he inquired to himself, "Who was at home? Was it me or someone else? Now I can return home and, insha'Allah, handle the challenges better."

IN PRACTICE

Self-control through willpower is essential. As humans, we have limitations on everything. If a person is sucked into an environment where he or she cannot be himself or herself, one of the suggestions is to change the environment. As in the preceding story, the Sufi altered his environment and hurried to the mosque to pray before his anger caused further damage. As soon as he engaged in a genuine relationship with Allah ﷾, he regained his normal, desired self. Once the individual regains this positive potential energy, he or she can return to life's challenges to aid others on their journeys.

76. The Unusual Men and the Rebellion

Everyone was advised not to go outside due to the risk of frostbite and freezing, as a result of an extreme cold warning. The streets were empty with the exception of a few peculiar men. The Sufi gazed through the window. He recognized these individuals. Those individuals would not normally walk outside, but in times of storms and difficulty, they would do so to demonstrate their resilience and defiance. The Sufi smiled and wished, "I wish they would act rationally and heed the warnings." In these extreme cold temperatures, organs and life can be lost in a few seconds.

In practice

It is essential to follow guidelines. Due to their rebellious nature, there are some individuals who may disobey instructions and instead do the opposite. Similarly, when Allah ﷻ established dos and don'ts in relation to Himself, there would still be those who disobeyed. In this situation, it is extremely risky to be in the opposite position, as it can ruin one's life both in this world and the next.

77. Natural Disasters and Important Places

One day, the Sufi learned that a severe storm was imminent. Everyone was going to the market to purchase additional food while watching the news about the impending disaster. The Sufi dashed to the mosque immediately to pray. She remained in the mosque until the disaster had passed. Everyone was stressed and anxious, but the Sufi was calm and content. The Sufi said "Alhamdulillah."

IN PRACTICE

If a person knows how to handle adversity, overcoming it is simple. In the preceding story, the Sufi followed the example of Rasulullah ﷺ, who would pray until a potential disaster or calamity passed.[6][5] People may not always know how to respond to disasters. As there are physical preparations to be made, such as purchasing food or inspecting candles in case of a power outage, the individual may also be preparing themselves spiritually to connect with Allah ﷻ, Who is All-Powerful and Who can change anything.

78.   Irregular Prayers of Difficulty and the Sufi

The Sufi was in the mosque one day. She realized there was a person in her life who never attended the mosque but only did so in times of difficulty. The individual consulted the Sufi for advice. The Sufi told her, "I wish you would visit me on a regular basis, not just when you're in trouble, as this would provide you with more courage, hope, and coping mechanisms."

IN PRACTICE

Regular, small steps are more significant than irregular, giant leaps. In other words, a person may practice extreme religiosity once or twice per month for one week. Another person may practice religiosity a few minutes per day. As suggested by the Prophet, spiritual strength and stability would be greater in the second option than in the first.[6]xii

79. The Lonely Wise-Fool

There was a lonely wise-fool who frequented the mosque. Everyone would make jokes about him. A few weeks passed before he returned to the mosque. Then, on a particularly cold day, he arrived at the mosque. He was not appropriately attired to withstand the frigid weather. People warned him not to go outside without gloves or a coat, as he could become ill or even die otherwise. The wise-fool became enraged and exclaimed, "I've been at home for a long time and no one has asked me anything. Why are you concerned with me now?"

In practice

As we are all human, it is essential to check on people. People become lonely, depressed, and in need of companionship. A simple phone call or brief visit can avert tremendous spiritual depressions and impasses.

80.   Nights, Sleep, and Dreams

One day, the Sufi awoke with great unease. She was troubled by the amount of time she spent and how much of it she wasted by sleeping. She did not want to waste her remaining time sleeping and doing nothing because she was getting older. Then, she shared her problem with her teacher. Her teacher instructed her, "Before going to sleep, read some chants, and as soon as you wake up, begin reciting chants and praising Allah ﷻ." Then, hopefully, you will feel better, and the time spent reciting chants before and after sleep will be regarded as worship by Allah ﷻ while you are sleeping."

In practice

In the pursuit of establishing a relationship with Allah ﷻ, it is essential to value time as it pertains to one's own time. Before sleeping, Rasulullah ﷺ suggested reciting phrases such as 33 times SubhanAllah and 33 times Alhamdulillah. As a simulation of death, the person's final act of life would be an effort to connect with Allah ﷻ before falling asleep. Likewise, Rasulullah ﷺ would say, "Thank you, Allah ﷻ, for bringing us back to life after our death, the sleep."[6]

81.   Guidance, Uncertainty, and the Journey

The Sufi awoke one morning and thought to herself, "People believe I am religious and spiritual." She pondered the spiritual journey and her own death. She felt fearful and uneasy regarding the uncertainty of completing the journey with death. Then, she immediately added on her prayer list one of the prayers of Rasulullah. ﷺ "Oh Allah ﷻ, do not cause our hearts to stray after You have guided us, and grant us Your Infinite Mercy and Blessing. Indeed, You are the Generous and Endless Giver of All Blessings and Gifts. Amen!"[xiii]

IN PRACTICE

Positive uncertainty is referred to as the path's safety measure.[6] If this safeguard is not present, a person can easily become trapped in spiritual chasms. In other words, when a person believes and feels, "I am secure and safe" this is the point of no return. Therefore, when beginning a journey, a person should constantly ask Allah ﷻ to keep them on the straight path, as suggested in the Qur'an and in the prayers of the Prophet.

---

6. Tamken.

82.   Being with Old Friends, the Journey, and the Progress

The Sufi visited her old Sufi friends one day. During the journey, they were conversing about Sufi-related topics, and she was enjoying herself. The Sufi realized that the spiritual level of her old friends has not changed. When the Sufi expressed her perspective on the topic under discussion, her friends realized that she had reached a much higher level. The Sufi then exclaimed, "Astagfirullah, this could be a trap!"

IN PRACTICE

It is essential to desire spiritual advancement in one's relationship with Allah . On the journey, everyone travels at varying speeds. Some may not make significant progress, but they preserve what they have. Some will return. Some will remain despite little progress. Some will excel significantly in the journey's race. Consistent self-reflection, repentance, gratitude, and humility towards Allah ﷻ is crucial. If not, the progress itself may contain traps or holes that the individual may not realize are there. Some of these holes may be arrogance, superiority, or vanity. In this perspective, when the Sufi realized her error, she immediately asked Allah ﷻ for forgiveness and repentance by saying "astagfirullah."

83. The Divorce

The Sufi was upset with his children and family one day. He awoke in the morning and told himself, "I should not be angry because it is the weekend and everyone is at home." He then decided to leave his home and visit the mosque to pray for spiritual fortitude and divine assistance. The mosque was empty with the exception of a man the Sufi had never seen before. The man was also praying. After completing the prayer the Sufi engaged the man in conversation. The man stated, "I am undergoing a divorce. Please perform dua and pray for me." The man had been married for 22 years and was the father of seven children. The Sufi attempted to advise the man on how to save his marriage. The man stated, "I wish to escape and be with Allah ﷻ. Before I die, I wish to accomplish my goals. I am 55 years old." The Sufi responded, "Okay, you may be a shadow man at home, maintain your marriage, and still devote your time to the worship of Allah ﷻ." The individual insisted it was impossible. The Sufi thought to himself, "SubhanAllah, Allah ﷻ has sent me someone who will assist me and be patient with my problems."

IN PRACTICE

It is always recommended to seek refuge in Allah ﷻ during times of difficulty and distress. The man and the Sufi both ran to the mosque to pray and seek assistance. Due to the fact that the man was going through a divorce, the Sufi drew a lesson from his circumstance. Whenever possible, it is essential to avoid undesirable events like divorce. If all other options have failed, Allah ﷻ permits divorce, but it should be the last resort, not the first. It is essential to recognize that it is possible to worship and spend time with Allah ﷻ while maintaining social and familial obligations, despite the fact that it may be difficult at times. Therefore, it is preferable to maintain both, without sacrificing either.

84.   The Woman in the Graveyard

The Sufi visited a cemetery outside the city one day. The cemetery was situated away from the town. The Sufi traveled there to pay respects to a deceased friend. There was only one woman walking through the cemetery. It was uncommon to see an individual without a car walking through the cemetery. The Sufi went to his friend's graveside. He recited some prayers and the Yasin chapter of the Qur'an. After finishing, the Sufi began walking to his car. The Sufi began to drive. Once more, the Sufi observed the woman walking. The Sufi thought to himself, "Let me see if she's okay." When he stopped his car next to her and asked, "Are you okay?" she removed her sunglasses. There were tears, and she responded, "Yes, I visit my father several times per week and speak with him." The Sufi apologized for disturbing then drove away.

IN PRACTICE

It is essential to visit and pray for the deceased. There are individuals in higher spiritual states who are aware of the deceased's affairs in the afterlife. There are instances in which Rasulullah ﷺ reported what a person was doing in their grave while visiting or passing a cemetery.[6]xiv [5]xv Rasulullah ﷺ also stated that when someone visits a grave and greets the deceased, the deceased hears but is unable to respond.

85. Gourmet Coffee Making

The Sufi was in a good spiritual state one day. Today, she thought to herself, I'll make gourmet coffee. While chanting, she first reflected on the aroma and flavor of the coffee. After some time, she placed the coffee in the machine, poured water into its container, and chanted over it. Then, before brewing the coffee, she opened the coffee machine's lid and began smelling the coffee. The coffee smelled exceptionally good. She delighted in the aroma of the coffee while she chanted on it for a few moments. Then she said "bismillah" and pressed the button for the switch. As the coffee was brewing, a pleasant aroma of coffee emanated, which the Sufi enjoyed while chanting. The drips of coffee into the coffee pot, the aroma of freshly brewed coffee, and the chants of praise and thanksgiving for Allah ﷻ were all extremely enjoyable. The final drop then entered the coffee pot. The coffee pot was filled to capacity. Now, the Sufi was contemplating the deliciously fresh coffee. How she would consume the coffee and how it would travel through her mouth, throat, and stomach. It contains no calories, so she felt no guilt. The Sufi then took her first sip while she continued to chant. It was an experience beyond description!

In practice

It is essential to pay attention to every aspect of spiritual engagement. One may refer to this as awareness, mindfulness, or presence. When travelers adhere to the fundamental guidelines established by the Qur'an and the Prophet, the scholars describe their experiences. Over time, a spiritual science with a methodology that has been utilized for centuries develops.

86. Alone in the Cemetery

The Sufi desired to attend a funeral one day. Unfortunately, he missed the funeral prayer, but he vowed to attend at least the burial in the cemetery. As he was busy that day, he left his work to drive to the cemetery, which was located far away. By the time he reached the cemetery, the burial was complete and all but a few individuals had left. The Sufi parked and walked to the newly-dug grave; everyone else left the cemetery but him. The Sufi saluted the deceased and reflected on past memories and how he used to converse with him. The Sufi felt sad and began to read prayers and Qur'anic chapters, particularly the chapter of Yasin. The Sufi then said his farewells to his friend in the grave and left the cemetery.

IN PRACTICE

As evidenced by the Prophet, it is highly rewarded by Allah ﷻ to attend the funeral prayers and burial ceremony in the cemetery.[6]xvi [5]xvii This is due to remembering death and taking responsibility for one's actions prior to death. Or, people may tend to avoid sad events such as funerals in favor of more enjoyable activities. Therefore, when a person attends a funeral or burial ceremony in a cemetery, Allah ﷻ rewards them for carrying out their duty to their loved ones. As the Prophet testified, it is also recommended to salute the deceased when entering and exiting the cemetery, as the deceased can hear but cannot speak.[5] As in the preceding story, the deceased person is grateful for the visitors, especially when they pray to Allah ﷻ for him or her.

87.   Two Dogs, the Old Fox, and the Fish

The Sufi had a dream one day. Two dogs, an old fox, and a gentle fish were present. The o ld fox was attacked by the first dog. The old fox attempted to defend himself, but it was extremely challenging. The fox was old, frail, and underweight. The second dog then attacked the peaceful fish that had landed on the shore. The fish attempted to defend itself, but it was futile; the dog had already begun eating the fish, but the fish continued to try to defend itself. The Sufi awoke from the dream in the middle of the night, startled and uneasy. The following day, the Sufi went to her teacher to inquire about the meanings. Her instructor stated, "The fox is your husband. The fish represents you. Your dog is your child. Your husband must employ the fox's intelligence and astuteness when interacting with the children. In addition, it appears the children may be mistreating you. You and your husband must collaborate to prevent this and raise your children with discernment as a team. As depicted in the dream, the children have a lot of energy because the dogs want to attack and eat them. Allah always knows the best and most accurate meanings." The Sufi then approached her husband for advice.

In practice

It is essential to interpret dreams' messages. Rasulullah ﷺ would inquire after the early morning prayer[xviii] if anyone had dreams that required interpretation.[6][xix] Depending on time, context, and a person's spiritual state, there are a variety of criteria for a genuine and authentic dream. Authentic dreams are additional signs from Allah ﷻ. It is essential to seek the interpretation of one's dreams from experts in the field and from those who will always act in the individual's best interest.

88. Driving and Moving Objects

The Sufi was driving one day. She looked out the window of her home. She thought to herself, "It appears that things are moving." She stopped then. The road was blocked by a large rock. Let me try to move this rock, she said. She attempted for several minutes without success. She thought, "Well, I can't move this rock in this position. Let me attempt to reverse my vehicle and return to locate another side road." As she drove with the transmission in reverse, she observed that the rock appeared to be moving away from her. She told herself, "If I can't push something away from me, I'll move away from it. The outcome is the same."

In practice

It is essential to change environments and associate with positive people. Similar to how difficult it was to move the rock in the preceding story, it is sometimes very difficult to change oneself. Changing environments, such as "moving on" to the positive environments of dhikr, Allah⬥'s remembrance, and prayers, can bring about a change in oneself. This method is sometimes simple and yields the same result.

89. Fame

One day, the Sufi pondered, "Why is fame so harmful? I believe fame can be utilized for positive purposes. If a person is well-known, he or she can do good deeds for others and be imitated." Then, she contemplated Satan. Satan is the most well-known. I do not wish to be as famous as Satan. The Sufi then asked, "What is the definition of fame?"

IN PRACTICE

Everything is carried out with the sole intention of pleasing Allah ﷻ. The Oxford dictionary[2] defines fame as "the state of being known or talked about by many people, especially because of outstanding accomplishments." Asking for fame is ineffective and potentially dangerous. Therefore, there are many Sufis who deliberately avoid the path to fame. They wish to live and be buried in anonymity, known only to Allah ﷻ and not to people. Maintaining sincerity on the path in one's relationship with Allah ﷻ becomes extremely difficult if a person attains fame without desiring or seeking it. It is possible, but not easy.

90.   The Bad News Giver: Did You Know What Happened?

One day, the Sufi witnessed a man inside the mosque. This man's title according to the Sufi was "bad news bearer." Each time he saw him, the Sufi would inform him of tragic events by asking, "Did you hear what happened?" Then, for instance, he would report, "There was an accident on the highway, and people were killed." Or, "A snowstorm is expected tonight, and there is a traffic ban," along with other bad news. Every time the Sufi heard about it, he would continue to pray, chant, and meditate without being disturbed.

In practice

It is essential to be prepared for the outcomes of one's life journey. Someone once asked Rasulullah ﷺ, "When is the end of the world and the day of reckoning before Allah ﷻ?" Rasulullah responded by asking, "How did you prepare for it?"[5] In one's relationship with Allah ﷻ, it is more important to have a schedule than to elaborate on the unseen or unexpected events known as "news." Consequently, a person who has reached a spiritual level of neutrality[xx] is not greatly affected by news of evil or seemingly good events.

91.   Allah ﷻ, Humans, and Lies

One day, the Sufi pondered the best way to pray to Allah ﷻ. She first uttered some divine phrases of glorification,[7] appreciation,[8] and proclamation of Allah ﷻ's[9] Oneness and Uniqueness, and then asked for forgiveness.[10] In the second phase of her prayer, she asked Allah ﷻ to grant her the good she desired for this life and the next. She began and concluded her prayer by saluting and thanking all teachers, particularly the Prophet.[xxi] The Sufi then stated, "Allah ﷻ is Perfect, the Creator, with no requirements. Humans are the only creatures with needs and frailties.

In practice

It is essential to understand the limits of one's relationship with Allah ﷻ. Allah ﷻ is not like humans, despite the fact that we sometimes use analogies to make things more understandable in human communication. These similes and metaphors are acceptable so long as the user is aware that they are just that. These are the perimeters. Passing the limits of the human mind can put a person at risk of confusion, not genuine knowledge, and the loss of mind and heart. As in the preceding story, there are proper ways to pray to Allah ﷻ. First, one proclaims the truths and facts about Allah ﷻ with Divine Phrases of glorification, appreciation, and the Oneness and Uniqueness of Allah ﷻ, followed by a request for forgiveness. As a sign of gratitude, one can then ask for their needs while always remembering Rasulullah and other teachers at the beginning and end of the prayer. The Divine Phrases are filled with information about Allah ﷻ. If it were applied to humans, it would be a lie because humans are fragile and in need. Therefore, human arrogance is the greatest fault before Allah ﷻ.

---

7. SubhanAllah
8. Alhamdulillah
9. La ilaha illa Allah
10. Astagfirullah

92. Silence and Talking

One day, the Sufi attended a spiritual gathering. There was a person with a difficult life who was present at this gathering. The discussion centered on the concept of fate and one's relationship with Allah ﷻ. Although the Sufi was holding himself in a state of silence, there was a misunderstanding regarding the concept of theodicy, so he felt compelled to explain the ideal expected disposition of a person during these discussions. After leaving this gathering, he felt uncomfortable. He thought to himself, "I hope I did not imply anything that would make that person even more guilty. I wish I hadn't spoken, as I had promised myself previously."

In practice

It is extremely difficult to maintain a balance between speaking and silence. Before speaking, it is expected that a person has thoughtfully considered his or her thoughts. Using a language and voice tone without irritating others is comparable to heat, fire, or an oven in this instance. Empathy for others is the spice of conversation. However, the primary purpose of communication is to address one's own self or ego in order to improve it, not the other person. In this regard, the Sufi had a difficult time balancing all of these crucial elements, as described in the preceding narrative.

93. Finding Yourself

One day, the Sufi was contemplating the concept of self-awareness. She pondered, "How can I understand myself?" She pondered the response to this question for many years. She had a very busy life. Over the years, she changed her schedule and began spending more time alone, praying, reading the Qur'an, and engaging in soul searching. As time passed in these moments of solitude, she began to discover what makes her happy, what makes her sad, what makes her body uncomfortable and what makes it comfortable, etc. She said to herself one day, "Now, I believe I am discovering myself."

IN PRACTICE

It is crucial to understand who you are. If a person knows oneself, this is the first step toward knowing Allah ﷻ and developing a genuine relationship with the Divine. In the solitary moments of prayers, reading the Qur'an, and recitations, a person seeks to discover his or her true self under the guidance of Allah ﷻ via the Qur'an and the Prophet. In practice, it is essential to treat oneself or ego[11] as if it were a distinct individual. As a person comes to know another over time, so too can it take time to come to know oneself. Once a person knows themselves, he or she can move on to training the self or ego.

---

11. Called nafs in practice.

94. Astagfirullah

One day, the Sufi's heart began to feel uneasy. She felt discomfort. Then, she began to chant the phrase astagfirullah and began to cry. A few minutes later, the Sufi began to feel better. She said "alhamdulillah, thank you Allah ﷻ."

IN PRACTICE

When a person's heart is troubled, he or she can recite the phrase astagfirullah, which translates to "oh Allah ﷻ, please forgive me for all my actions with my eyes, ears, organs, mind, heart, thoughts, and feelings." Rasulullah ﷺ says, "There are times when I feel a shadow in my heart, and I seek Allah ﷻ's forgiveness a hundred times a day." [2] xxii Although Rasulullah ﷺ had a very close and unbroken relationship with Allah ﷻ even during his sleep, and was constantly protected and guided by Allah ﷻ, he also asked Allah ﷻ for forgiveness as a human for any possible errors. In the preceding narrative, the Sufi did not know the origin of the problem, but he immediately attempted to resolve it by employing this chant. It is essential to be conscious of one's heart. As a means of purifying one's heart, a person should remove any undesirable emotions, thoughts, or interpretations by asking for forgiveness. In practice, it is well known that asking Allah ﷻ for forgiveness purifies the heart, particularly with the chant astagfirullah.

95.   Loud and Silent

One day, the Sufi participated in a meditation and chanting circle. The crowd was chanting loudly. The following day, the Sufi attended another meditation and chanting circle. People were silently chanting. The Sufi thought to herself, "Wow, a person can choose a behavior based on their mental and emotional state of the day."

IN PRACTICE

Meditation and chanting can be performed either loudly or in silence. In both instances, there are potential benefits. When a person is in a group that is chanting loudly, the audible medium can provide spiritual uplift. When a person is surrounded by a group chanting in silence, they can experience the spiritual uplift of the sensible medium. One should keep in mind that chanting at a high volume can sometimes be disadvantageous because it makes it difficult for others to concentrate. As Rasulullah ﷺ once reminded the people, Allah ﷻ is All-Hearing, All-Present, and Close, so they should refrain from shouting when reciting the Quran. Allah ﷻ is constantly with the individual.[2] xxiii

96.   Going Back and Back

One day, the Sufi committed an act that was considered a sin or an affront to Allah ﷻ. He previously promised himself he would not do it again, but he did it again. He felt embarrassed in the presence of Allah ﷻ. Allah ﷻ gave him a great deal. He asked himself, "How could I confront Allah ﷻ?" He went off to pray. Then he began to cry and begged for forgiveness, saying, "Oh Allah! Where should I go? No one can forgive my disrespectful and impolite treatment of You. Please pardon me. You are the Most Merciful Person. You are the Most Merciful and Compassionate Being."

IN PRACTICE

It is essential to return to Allah ﷻ repeatedly until death. Allah ﷻ is the only one who can help a person in reality. If Allah ﷻ wills and accepts, then other means will follow. If Allah ﷻ does not wish to accept a person, even if others appear to comfort them, there is in reality no one who can assist them. In the preceding story, the Sufi embodied a prayer suggested by the Prophet: "Oh, My Sustainer and Nourisher, I have repeatedly rebelled against You by committing sins. No one but You can forgive those sins. Please forgive me as You have forgiven me. Be merciful to me. Indeed, You are the Most Merciful and Gracious, the Most Forgiving, and the Most Accepting of Repentance."[2] xxiv

97.   Pain and Mistakes

One day, the Sufi reflected on the errors he had committed in his relationship with Allah ﷻ. Each time he did something wrong to harm the relationship, he experienced excruciating remorse and guilt. Then, he attempted to limit his pessimism so as not to lose his relationship with Allah ﷻ. "It is very difficult to maintain balance on the path," he reflected.

In practice

In one's relationship with Allah ﷻ, it is vital to return and seek forgiveness for one's evil-seeming portrayals of others. There is no limit on the number of times one can return because, in reality, no one can return except Allah ﷻ. Positive emotions are accompanied by self-responsibility and unpleasant emotions disgust for oneself. Occasionally, a person may face perilous temptations and become unsure about returning to Allah ﷻ. This is a very perilous path that a person can cross resulting in succumbing to evil temptations that cause them to view themselves as losers and become pessimistic in their relationship with Allah ﷻ. Self-accountability with modesty and humility should be balanced with a firm belief that Allah ﷻ's mercy is infinite and that Allah ﷻ can forgive anyone, regardless of the gravity of his or her sins.

98. In Charge

One day, the Sufi contemplated the immensity of leadership responsibilities. "I have control over my tongue, body, and mind. I am responsible for my kids. I am responsible for responsibilities in both my professional and personal lives. Too many tasks and responsibilities make it difficult to manage everything."

IN PRACTICE

It is undesirable to have control over something or someone. However, if a person is given a responsibility despite avoiding it, it is expected that they will fulfill it as satisfactorily as possible. Being accountable to people and Allah ﷻ for something or someone is a consequence of being in charge of it or them. One's relationship with Allah ﷻ can reach a very high level if he or she is a good, just leader or a loving spouse. In contrast, oppression and unjust treatment in family life can make one's accountability before Allah ﷻ challenging and difficult.

99.   Intention and Difficulties

One day, the Sufi attended a challenging religious event. He neglected to communicate his intent before attending. During this gathering, religious topics were discussed in an impolite manner. The Sufi attempted to contribute his "two cents" but was uncertain whether they would be useful. As usual, the Sufi did not feel well and left. He questioned, "Why did I come here?"

IN PRACTICE

Prior to taking any action, it is vital to establish your purpose. Even when things appear straightforward, it is necessary to renew and reaffirm one's intention to obtain the greatest benefit. Unexpectedly unpleasant circumstances may arise from time to time. If the person has a good intention in these situations, Allah ﷻ will still reward them due to their intention. In the preceding story, the Sufi's problem was that he forgot to make an intention before attending the gathering. When he encountered a challenging and unpleasant environment, he recalled his intention to seek comfort and relief, but he realized that he had not made an intention prior to going.

100. Jury Duty

One day, the Sufi was summoned to serve on a jury. Like everyone else, she attended court. There were many potential jurors waiting in the room for the initial selection process. It appeared that the majority of those present did not wish to be there and hoped the judge would excuse them. The Sufi asked herself, "How can I isolate myself from my surroundings and transform this room into my place of worship?" The Sufi then prayed to Allah ﷻ for this transformation and began engaging in her prayers while she waited for several hours. Others were complaining, but the Sufi praised Allah ﷻ for this transformation by saying "Alhamdulillah."

IN PRACTICE

It is important to realize one's physical conditions and accordingly ask from Allah ﷻ the means for spiritual transformation. Sometimes, it is difficult to disconnect oneself from one's surroundings due to various distractions, although it is not impossible. Making the intention and asking help from Allah ﷻ are the key first steps as the Sufi did in the above story. After, one can engage oneself with chanting, prayers, and readings. If the person is flowing in this engagement, the transformation is successful. That is great. If not, the person should not force themselves but possibly refresh themselves with wudhu, or pick a chant that is easy to recite.

101. Lawsuits and Ethics

One day, the Sufi was summoned to serve on a jury. The case involved a lawsuit. The Sufi was unfamiliar with lawsuits and felt negatively about it. He always believed that lawsuits were an unfair method of obtaining money from individuals. Then he told the judge, "I believe I have a prejudice against lawsuits." The judge asked why. The Sufi stated, "I do not believe that people intentionally commit wrongdoing and indifference." The judge announced, "You are excused from jury duty." The Sufi then began to reflect and asked himself, "Did I do something correctly? What if there are necessary legal actions" He kept pondering . . .

IN PRACTICE

It is essential to think before speaking. The Sufi's position on lawsuits was uncertain until the judge excused him from jury duty. Then, he began to elaborate on it. Unjust accumulation of wealth is one of the most pressing concerns for Allah ﷻ. When it becomes the norm in a society, despite its popularity, it poses a threat to the social, ethical, and religious pillars. On the other hand, lawsuits can prompt individuals to evaluate their practices. Self-improvement can be referred to as checks and balances on the spiritual path. Consequently, in this instance, lawsuits can be advantageous in social life as a means of engaging in self-reflection.

102. Sleep and Complications

Recently, the Sufi had sleep problems. As he awoke, he felt ill and continued to have headaches and bad dreams. Again, it was night, and the Sufi was preparing for sleep. He thought to himself, "When I awaken with pain, I will once again be in pain. What am I to do? Should I see a physician?" Then, before going to bed, he recalled the prophetic advice and used the restroom to relieve himself, performed wudhu, washed his hands, went to bed and began reading some prayers. He eventually fell asleep on his right side. He had a pleasant dream and felt great in the morning, so he said "alhamdulillah."

IN PRACTICE

To relieve oneself of the burden of decision-making, it is essential to follow the Prophetic advice in every aspect of life. In other words, when a person must make important life decisions without the Prophet's guidance, he or she may make decisions that are unnecessary and counterproductive. In this instance of sleep, prior to consulting a physician or requesting medical assistance, the Sufi remembered to follow the Prophetic recommendations regarding proper sleeping habits. With the help of the Prophet's simple and blessed advice, he was able to avoid the hassle of medical appointments. This does not imply that medical assistance should not be sought when necessary; however, sometimes a simple approach can resolve a problem without complications.

103. Throat and Silence

There once was a Sufi who never spoke in the morning. When he would visit the mosque, he would maintain silence until the afternoon. When people attempted to speak with him, he would expose his throat and use sign language to communicate. As time progressed, some brothers became concerned about the Sufi's throat. They approached the Sufi and attempted to give him herbal medicine and lengthy advice on how he should take better care of his health. The Sufi listened attentively and nodded his head. The Sufi thought to himself, "Perhaps I should have told them that I don't want to speak in the morning, but then they would have thought I was strange."

IN PRACTICE

In practice, there are travelers on the path who do not wish to engage with worldly concerns until the morning, when they have been charged with spiritual equipment. The Sufi in the preceding narrative was one of them. The Sufi did not wish to speak and preferred silence until a certain time of day. However, he did not wish to share this information with others. Sometimes it is difficult to appear normal around others when one dislikes speaking to others. It is more important not to be affected by people feeling superior and arrogant if you receive unwanted disturbance from others due to your abnormal behavior.

104. Coffee Cup Taste vs. Size

A generous Sufi used to offer complimentary light coffee in small cups. The coffee was so weak that it resembled water in flavor. As soon as they took a sip, people would exclaim, "This is the best espresso I have ever tasted." The Sufi would tell each individual that it was light coffee and not expresso. Later, she grew weary of correcting others on this matter. Now, whenever someone says, "This is the best espresso I've ever had," she smiles and tells herself, "Everyone is fooled by the size of the cup."

IN PRACTICE

It is essential not to be fooled by appearances. Since expresso coffee is served in small cups, people assumed and judged that the light coffee they were drinking was expresso even after tasting it. Occasionally, our judgments are so strong that there are clear guidelines, yet we act without consideration. Likewise, on the spiritual path, knowing Allah ﷻ and destroying all negative or incorrect judgments can be difficult, but not impossible. When some people hear the words Allah ﷻ or religion, they may immediately be compelled by preconceived notions, regardless of what is being presented.

105. Spiritual Discoveries

A Sufi used to attend a lecture given by another Sufi at night. During the day, the first Sufi would focus on a variety of heart and mind-related issues. She would pray, reflect, and record her spiritual discoveries. At night, when the other Sufi was giving a public lecture, she would reference the first Sufi's spiritual discoveries. Over time, the first Sufi normalized this and told herself, "By the Grace of Allah ﷻ, the abnormal becomes the norm in spiritual life."

IN PRACTICE

It is essential to understand that Allah ﷻ can bestow spiritual insights and revelations upon a person who is attempting to maintain steadfastness and perseverance on the path. On this trip, things that are abnormal for others may become normal for this traveler. In a prophetic tradition, it is stated that Allah ﷻ commands one of the angels[12] to provide the correct inspiration when a person walks the path with humility. All of these insights and discoveries are the result of Allah ﷻ's grace. The individual should be cautious and modest. Due to these spiritual discoveries and blessings, he or she should not fall prey to the temptations of superiority.

---

12. Name of the angel is mulhim.

106. Sufi's Prayer and Regret

There was once a poor but devout Sufi. There were family friends who frequently visited her. The Sufi began to experience severe and intolerable family issues. The Sufi then prayed to Allah ﷻ, "Oh Allah ﷻ, take care of whoever is causing these problems." Then, after some time, she learned that the family friend who had been coming to her house and causing issues with her family was undergoing a divorce. The Sufi asked herself, "What have I done?" I wish that you didn't pray."

IN PRACTICE

It is extremely risky to make the friends of Allah ﷻ sad and upset. They do nothing but pray to Allah ﷻ for help with their difficulties. In this regard, people have generally been very cautious when interacting with the friends of Allah ﷻ, whose prayers are instantly accepted due to their high standing with Allah ﷻ. In the preceding story, the Sufi had a family member who regularly caused her family problems by visiting their home. The Sufi then prayed to Allah ﷻ, and although her prayer was answered, she was upset with herself.

107. Loving-Warning and the Traffic Ticket

One day, while driving, the Sufi was contemplating a Sufi teacher. The Sufi had negative feelings about this Sufi teacher regarding an issue. A police car flashed its lights behind the Sufi's vehicle as soon as he became preoccupied with these thoughts while driving. As expected, the Sufi received a ticket, and he thought to himself, "It's not surprising that I receive a ticket whenever I have negative thoughts about a teacher."

IN PRACTICE

Regarding the teachers of Allah ﷻ, it is important to control oneself, including one's thoughts. Occasionally, if there are two people who are both friends of Allah ﷻ, there may be some loving admonitions for the one who may not have good feelings towards the other. This loving-warning may be in the form of a traffic ticket or a negative occurrence that may disrupt the individual's life flow. In such situations, one should be grateful to Allah ﷻ because he or she has received a loving-warning, analogous to the relationship between a child and a mother. Allah ﷻ is superior to all of these depictions, but a person can humanize evil-appearing occurrences encountered in life.

108. Intellectualizing the Religion and the Etiquettes

One day, the Sufi pondered intellectuals and their fundamental premise of employing the mind. She told herself, "Up to a certain point, one can use their mind. The essence is the attitude of courtesy and respect, not the intellect."

In practice

This is the central point: the essence of religion is a disposition of courtesy and reverence[13] for Allah ﷻ. If a person lacks the boundaries of etiquette, then it is very easy for him or her to mentally and emotionally wander around in poisonous mindsets similar to black holes in space. The chant SubhanAllah constantly reminds the individual of this fact. These errant wanderings necessitate constant corrections and repentance with the astagfirullah chant. When a person reaches this level of understanding, it is recommended that they thank Allah ﷻ for this spiritual level by reciting alhamdulillah. As the Prophet reminded us, knowing the guidelines of the path is essential, as is knowledge that is useful and beneficial.[5] These are the primary areas where philosophers and some religious people in the West may have problems due to a lack of: 1) etiquette with Allah ﷻ; 2) knowledge of one's limitations as a human in this relationship; and 3) acceptance and submission to the guidelines as cornerstones.

---

13. Adab

109. Proud Sufi

The Sufi was reading the Qur'an one day. He read the verses[xxv] concerning the reasons why Allah sent humans as messengers rather than angels. Allah stated that if angel messengers were to be sent, they would take the form of humans. The Sufi then asked himself, "Why are people not content with being human and desire something else? I am honored to be a human. Thank you Allah ﷻ, alhamdulillah."

In practice

Accepting yourself is the first step toward success. In this case, humans are weak, dependent, and Allah ﷻ's creations. Once a person maintains this perspective with humility and modesty, he or she can find strength in his or her human characteristics in his or her relationship with Allah ﷻ. The majority of issues arise when humans refuse to accept this reality in their relationship with the Creator. They attempt to conceal themselves with clothing, even when they are unaware. The worst attire is that of arrogance, superiority, and power when in reality the individual is weak, destitute, and impoverished. This falsehood puts the majority of people in conflict with Allah ﷻ in this life and the next.

110. True Gratitude

One day, the Sufi wondered, "Why can't I thank Allah entirely? It should be as effortless as breathing air into my lungs. It ought to be effortless."

In practice

Everything in practice begins with effort and imitation. Occasionally, a person may be thanking Allah ﷻ and saying Alhamdulillah, but still have stingy thoughts or inner friction. With time and practice, a natural disposition of gratitude can develop. The expressions "what a small number of thankers!"[xxvi] and "how small a toll for the habit of thanking"[xxvii] are repeated throughout the Qur'an to allude to human ingratitude and lack of appreciation for Allah ﷻ. Rasulullah ﷺ also indicates that "one who does not thank Allah ﷻ does not thank people"[12], or vice versa. Allah ﷻ increases a person's happiness and peaceful blessings in this world and the next if he or she is always thankful, alhamdulillah.

111. No Accountable Leaders

One day, a man traveled to a city. There were no people others could be held accountable to. People used to steal and kill at will. This man was startled and asked a local, "Why is there no leaders in this town?" The local resident stated, "No one wants to be the person responsible for enforcing rules and laws. Therefore, no one wants that job despite the fact that it pays off well."

IN PRACTICE

In one's relationship with Allah ﷻ, it is essential to observe rules and accept responsibility. Typically, we frequently hear, "I don't want to be the bad guy." Allah ﷻ is All Merciful, Caring, and Loving in one's relationship with Him. One must acknowledge that there are individuals of varying levels. A person with a higher status would obey Allah﷽'s commands because he or she loves Allah ﷻ. Due to accountability after death, another person, possibly of a lower status, would obey Allah﷽'s commands. Both are acceptable and suitable. What is unacceptable is portraying Allah ﷻ as "Loving" but not "Accountable." This singular perspective can lead individuals of various levels to adopt the same attitude as those in the preceding story.

112. Good Deeds and Language

A man entered the mosque and began conversing with a man seated there. The man spent a few minutes listing the good deeds he had performed in the past for the sake of Allah ﷻ. The other man was smiling and looking at this man's face. Eventually, the man stopped speaking. The other man apologized, "I'm sorry, I don't speak English!"

In practice

It is important to keep one's good deeds private if they were performed for Allah ﷻ's sake. Sincerity is a prerequisite for Allah ﷻ's pleasure. Sincerity necessitates the absence of others applauding one's words or actions. Therefore, it is considered unbelief when a person performs a good deed in order to be praised or recognized by others. It makes little difference whether people know it or not. People can say "excellent work!" Then, a deceptive and false sense of satisfaction may ensue. Yet, when Allah ﷻ is pleased with a person, there is satisfaction both in this life and the next. In the preceding story, the man had a pointless conversation regardless of whether or not the other person understood him.

113. People's Sensitivity and Culture

There was a Sufi who disliked morning conversations. When he would visit the mosque, he preferred silence. A man from a different culture visited the Sufi in the mosque one morning. This man greatly admired the Sufi. He was angry toward the Sufi. He asked him, "What have I done to you?" Why are you not conversing with me?" The Sufi gave him coffee and wrote on a piece of paper, "The Sufi loves him too, but he is too busy right now to speak." The man was still angry, but he continued to complain to the Sufi about the Sufi's silence. The Sufi maintained his silence, bowed his head, and listened to the man. After the man left, the Sufi said to himself, "I ought to be more culturally sensitive. Not everyone understands my actions."

IN PRACTICE

Silence is the default mode of a non-speaking individual. There are those on the path who prefer silence at various times of the day, such as in the mornings, until they complete their daily dialogue with Allah ﷻ called wird. During these times, the individual desires to focus solely on their relationship with Allah ﷻ, devoid of any external or internal distractions of the mind or heart. During these times, some Sufis are unable to pay complete attention to social etiquette due to the engagement of others. An outsider should always think positively of others, in this case the Sufi in the preceding story. Nonetheless, Sufis should attempt to recognize the cultural and social sensitivities of people in order to prevent further evil that could lead to more distress in the future.

114. Ant and the Sufi

There was an ant who was going for pilgrimage. A Sufi saw him and asked him:

Sufi: Where are you going?

Ant: To the holy sites.

The Sufi laughs and says:

Sufi: I don't think you will make it. The holy sites are a thousand miles away from where we are right now.

Ant: I know that, but I have the intention.

The Sufi felt so embarrassed by his responses that he asked the ant to be his teacher.

In practice

Intentions precede actions. If a person always intends what is good and beneficial, Allah ﷻ rewards them in accordance with their intention. If a person prays or donates to the poor with the intention of impressing others or gaining some worldly benefit, that person can obtain what she or he desires in the world, the tag. After death, the individual may be punished for acting insincerely. In addition, Sufis frequently observe nature, animals, and plants in an effort to advance their spiritual development.

115. One Dollar Coffee Machine

A poor Sufi was found in a mosque. He spent one dollar on a small coffee machine and placed it in the mosque. During his stay in the mosque, he drank coffee alone. If other people visited the mosque, he would give them the leftover coffee. People began to respect him because he was so generous and gave everyone coffee as time passed. The Sufi gained a reputation as the mosque's respectable coffee maker.

IN PRACTICE

Our egos are comparable to inexpensive coffee makers. As Allah ﷻ grants the ego responsibility and acknowledgement, it gains value. Power, responsibility, and positions bring esteem. If one wishes to be recognized by Allah ﷻ, he or she must maintain humility and reverence for the Divine.

116. Coffee Machine and Serving

As people entered the mosque, everyone requested coffee from the renowned Sufi coffee maker. The Sufi was becoming agitated. While he was praying, individuals approached him and requested coffee. He decided one day to place the coffee machine on the serving table outside. If people desire coffee, they can make it themselves without disturbing the Sufi. People began brewing their own coffee so as not to disturb the Sufi. The Sufi thought to himself, "It doesn't matter if someone steals the coffee maker; I can purchase another one. It is low-cost."

In practice

Our egos are like inexpensive coffee makers. If we don't hoard it for ourselves and instead use it to serve others in order to please Allah ﷻ, a lowly self can have great worth. If we attempt to confine our egos, disturbances will increase. Therefore, one must let it go in order to experience the joy and fulfillment of serving others.

117. Cookies and Scripture

One day, a Sufi was memorizing and reciting the Quran. He spent considerable time with the holy book. Then, he took a coffee break. As soon as he approached the coffee machine, he noticed his favorite cookie next to it. He thought to himself, "I am the only person in the mosque. Who delivered this cookie? I am aware that this cookie isn't local. It must be ordered online." He indulged in deep thinking . . .

IN PRACTICE

Sometimes, miracles can be called cookies. As one engages in practice, such as reading the Qur'an, memorization, prayer, or fasting, cookies may take on a variety of forms. The question is: Is the cookie nutritious? In other words, is it an encouragement from Allah ﷻ for the path? Or, is it a test or trial from Allah ﷻ to determine whether the individual on the path will be arrogant by claiming supernatural occurrences and attempting to be superior to other humans beings?

118. Sufi Argues with His Wife

One day, a Sufi was in an argument with his wife. During the fight he decided to discuss some of their marriage problems.

Sufi: We need to talk.

His wife: You are probably going to tell me how bad I am!

Sufi: Probably, you already told to your friends and my kids how bad I am, so you took the precedence. Congratulations!

His Wife: You claim to be a Sufi and you think about your reputation. Shame on you!

Sufi: You think you are pious. Please stop pretending to be pious and naïve.

The Sufi was now thinking. He said to himself, "I am heading toward a dead end. I am already receiving a lot of texts from her on my phone. If I don't say anything then she will think that she won and I will hear about it for the rest of my life." "What should I do?" Then, he said to his wife:

Sufi: I wanted to meet with you to tell you how much I appreciate you and I love you. That was the reason . . .

The argument was over. Sufi said, "Alhamdulillah (thanks to Allah ﷻ), that was a good thought that Allah gave it to me. I was heading toward a dead end."

IN PRACTICE

In Sufi marriages, the spouse always has the last word. The husband's position is to remain silent and passive in all disagreements, to forgive, to avoid making a fuss, and to move on.

119. The Best Voice

There was a man in the mosque who believed he had the greatest voice when he sang the call to prayer.[14] People would leave the mosque as soon as he began singing the prayer call so that they would not hear his voice until he was finished. They waited outside before returning. This man approached the Sufi in the mosque one day with a recording of a renowned prayer singer and asked, "Would you please listen to this recording and tell me who sings the prayer call better? Me or the other singer?"

IN PRACTICE

Occasionally, a person's spiritual diseases can become his or her personality if there is no one to point out his or her errors. Therefore, it is customary for friends, not wives or husbands, to point out one's errors rather than simply praising one's accomplishments. One Sufi states, "I adore a friend who cautions me about a scorpion on my chest. Why should I feel anger towards her?

---

14. Adhan.

120. Looking at the Mirror

There was an untidy Sufi who disliked looking in the mirror. When he used to look in the mirror, he would think, "My messy hair, untrimmed moustache, uncombed beard, and unironed shirts make me extremely uncomfortable."

IN PRACTICE

Similarly, our internal disorder is can appear ugly. Allah made each person physically attractive. Ugliness consists primarily of arrogance, hatred, anger, and envy. If the individual lacks mirrors to reflect on this, then this is the true issue.

ENDNOTES

i. Shukr
ii. [14:7]
iii. This is a famous saying in sufism. The relationship between wird and waridat.
iv. Hadith 3:31
v. Zuhd
vi. Kabah, Mecca, and Madina.
vii. Nafs Ammarah
viii. Hurriyah
ix. Book 2:221
x. [13:28]
xi. Hadith 2678
xii. Hadith 81:53
xiii. [3, 8]
xiv. Hadith 218
xv. Hadith 292
xvi. Hadith 1325
xvii. Hadith 945
xviii. Fajr or morning prayer
xix. Hadith 7047
xx. Zuhd
xxi. Salawat
xxii. Hadith 2702
xxiii. Hadith 2704
xxiv. Hadith 2705
xxv. [18:24]
xxvi. For example, [34,13]
xxvii. For example, [23,78]

BIBLIOGRAPHY

[1] Al-Ghazzali, M. *Al-Ghazzali on Knowing Yourself and Allah* ﷻ. Kazi Publications Inc., 2003.

[2] Vahide, S. *The Collection of Light.* ihlas nur publication, 2001.

[3] al-Ba'uniyyah, A. *The Principles of Sufism.* NYU Press, 2016.

[4] Kumek, Y. J. *Practical Mysticism: Sufi Journeys of Heart and Mind.* Kendall Hunt, 2018.

[5] Muslim, A. *Sahih Muslim,* translated by A. Siddiqui. Peace Vision. 1972.

[6] Al-Bukhari, M. *The Translation of the Meanings of Sahih Al-Bukhari.* Kazi Publications, 1986.

[7] Ozkan, T. Y. *A Muslim Response to Evil: S. N. on the Theodicy.* Routledge, 2016.

[8] Murad, K. *In The Early Hours: Reflections on Spiritual and Self Development.* Kube Publishing Ltd, 2013.

[9] U. P. Oxford, "Oxford Dictionaries," 2016, http://www.oxforddictionaries.com/us/definition/american_english/.

[10] Al-Ghazali, M. *Deliverance from Error.* Louisville: Fons Vitae, 2000.

[11] Ali, A. Y. *The Meaning of the Glorious Qurān.* Islamic Books, 1938.

[12] Dawud, A. *Sunan Abu Dawud.* Darussalam, 2008.

[13] Ashraf, M. M. K. 'Alī Thānvī, *The Path to Perfection: An Edited Anthology of the Spiritual Teachings of Hakīm Al-Umma Mawlānā Ashraf 'Alī Thānawī.* White Thread, 2005.

[14] Ibn Qayyim. I. K. *The Soul's Journey After Death.* Noah, 2018.

[15] Vandestra, M. *Human Souls Journey After Death In Islam.* Dragon Promedia, 2017.

[16] Hanbal, A. B. *Musnad Imam Ahmad Ibn Hanbal.* Dar-Us-Salam Publications, 2012.

[17] U. P. Oxford, "Oxford Dictionaries," 2016. [Online]. Available: http://www.oxforddictionaries.com/us/definition/american_english/.

[18] Al-Ghazali, M. *Deliverance from Error,* Louisville: Fons Vitae, 2000.

[19] Salamah-Qudsi, A. *Sufism and Early Islamic Piety: Personal and Communal Dynamics.* Cambridge University Press, 2018.

[20] Muslim, A. *Sahih Muslim* (translated by Siddiqui, A.). Peace Vision. 1972.

[21] Hanbal, A. B. *Musnad Imam Ahmad Ibn Hanbal.* Dar-Us-Salam Publications, 2012.

[22] Kumek, Y. J. *Practical Mysticism: Sufi Journeys of Heart and Mind.* Kendall Hunt, 2018.

[23] Ansar, A. *Peace of Mind and Healing Broken Lives.* Universal Mercy, 2010.

[24] Smith, J. I. and Y. Y. Haddad. *The Islamic Understanding of Death and Resurrection.* Oxford University Press, 2002.

[25] Dorothy, G. and J. L. Singer. *Handbook of Children and the Media.* SAGE, 2002.

[26] Ring, N.C. *Introduction to the Study of Religion.* New York: Orbis, 2007.

[27] Ozkan, T. Y. *A Muslim Response to Evil: S. N. on the Theodicy.* Routledge, 2016.

[28] Al-Bukhari, M. *The Translation of the Meanings of Sahih Al-Bukhari.* Kazi Publications, 1986.

[29] Al-Ansari, A. B. "Ahadith al-Shuyukh al-Thiqat," vol. 2, no. 322, pp. 875–876.

[30] Tamer, Georges. *Islam and Rationality: The Impact of Al-Ghazālī: Papers Collected on His 900th Anniversary.* Boston: BRILL, 2015.

[31] Geoffroy, Eric, and Roger Gaetani. *Introduction to Sufism: The Inner Path of Islam.* Bloomington, Ind: World Wisdom, 2010.

[32] Shah, Idries. *The Sufis.* London: The Octagon Press, 1999.

[33] Jamal, Azim, and Nido R. Qubein. *Life Balance: The Sufi Way.* Mumbai, India: Jaico Pub. House, 2000.

[34] Shah, I. *Learning How to Learn: Psychology and Spirituality in the Sufi Way.* Octagon Press Ltd., 1978.

[35] Heer, Nicholas, Kenneth L. Honerkamp, al-Tirmidhī M. A. Hakīm, Muhammad -H. Sulamī, and Muhammad -H. Sulamī. *Three Early Sufi Texts.* Louisville: Fons Vitae, 2009.

[36] Singh, David E. *Sainthood and Revelatory Discourse: An Examination of the Bases for the Authority of Bayan in Mahwi Islam.* Delhi: Regnum International, 2003.

[37] Darimi, I. *Sunan Darimi.* Dar Al Kitab, 1997.

[38] Bukhari, M.I. I. *Moral Teachings of Islam: Prophetic Traditions from Al-Adab Al-mufrad.* Rowman Altamira, 2003.

[39] Schimmel, Annemarie, and Friedrich Heiler. *Deciphering the Signs of Allah ﷻ: A Phenomenological Approach to Islam ; [to the Memory of Friedrich Heiler (1892–1967)].* Albany: State Uni. of New York Press, 1994.

[40] Stowasser, Barbara F. *The Day Begins at Sunset: Perceptions of Time in the Islamic World.* I.B.Tauris, 2014.

[41] Al-Qahtani, S. B. W. *Fortress Of Muslim.* Darussalam Publishers, 2018.

[42] Abū, Dā'ūd S.-A.-S, and Ahmad Hasan. *Sunan Abu Dawud.* New Delhi: Kitab Bhavan, 2012.

[43] al-Qushayri, Abu -Q, and Alexander D. Knysh. *Al-qushayri's Epistle on Sufism: Al-risala Al-Qushayriyya Fi 'ilm Al-Tasawwuf.* Reading: Garnet Publishing, 2007.

[44] Ibn Qayyim, I. K. *The Soul's Journey After Death.* Noah, 2018.

[45] Khan, M. A. *Encyclopaedia of Sufism: Sufism and Naqshbandi order.* Anmol Publications, 2003.

[46] Adonis. *Sufism and Surrealism.* Saqi, 2013.

[47] Muhaiyaddeen, M R. B. *Dhikr: The Remembrance of Allah ﷻ.* Narbeth, Pa: Fellowship Press, 1999.

[48] Abdullah, P. M. *ISLAMIC TASAWWUF: Shariah And Tariqah.* Adam Publishers & Distributors, 2001.

[49] Vaughan-Lee, Llewellyn. *Love is a Fire: The Sufi's Mystical Journey Home.* The Golden Sufi Center, 2000.

[50] I. Majah, *Sunan Ibn Majah,* Kazi Publications, 1993.

[51] A. R. A. Nisa, *Sunan Nisai,* Kazi Publications, 1997.

[52] A. Muslim, Sahih Muslim (translated by Siddiqui, A.), *Peace Vision,* 1972.

[53] M. Tirmizi, Jami At-Tirmizi, *Dar-us-Salam,* 2007.

[54] M. Al-Bukhari, *The translation of the meanings of Sahih Al-Bukhari,* Kazi Publications, 1986.

[55] M. i. `. A. K. Al-Tabrizi, Mishkat al Masabih, Beirut: Dar Ibn Hazm, 2003.

[56] SInternational, *The Qurān,* Abul-Qasim Publishing House, 1997.

[57] S. Abu-Dawud, Sunan Abu Dawud, *Riyadh: Darussalam,* 2008.

GLOSSARY

A'bd: worshipper, servant, or slave

Accountability: liability, especially in Sufism and in Abrahamic traditions, everyone has a free will or agency in this world but accountability for their actions in the afterlife in front of Allah ﷻ

Adab: good manners, esp. in the relationship with Allah ﷻ in Sufism

Adjective: attribute, a phrase describing a noun

Adonai: name of Allah ﷻ in Judaism

Affair: relationship

Agency: acting as an agent or a carrier with free will

Alhamdulillah: a chanted divine phrase of appreciation of Allah ﷻ or Allah

Alienating: isolating, separating, disconnecting

Alienating Images of Allah ﷻ: understandings about Allah ﷻ that disconnects person to establish a regular relationship with the Divine or to follow a religion

Allah (ﷻ): Allah سبحانه وتعالى. The expression سبحانه وتعالى read as Subhānahu wa Tā'la also abbreviated as SWT and written as also Allah (SWT) is an expression of respect when the Name of Allah is mentioned. Among these expressions many English translations, one can be "Allah is One, Unique and Perfect with all the Divine Attributes and Names, far beyond human's negative and wrong constructions and imaginations. All Glory Belongs to Allah, the Most Exalted, the Most Respected, and the Most High."

Allude: explain, refer

Anger: uncontrolled and chaotic human spiritual state

Aphorism: sayings, proverbs in a culture, society, or belief

Appreciate: thank

Appreciative: with capital A, Allah ﷻ

Arabic: language, especially the language of revelation of the Qurãn

Arrogance: feelings and actions of superiority

Ascension: rising, especially in Sufism increase of spiritual states in relationship with Allah ﷻ

Assert: claim

Astagfirullah: a divine phrase of asking forgiveness from Allah ﷻ and cleaning the heart

Attribute: adjective, a phrase describing a noun, especially in Sufism, attributes of Allah ﷻ: divine phrases describing Allah ﷻ

Authentic: original, genuine, true

Balance: modesty, especially in Sufism, following the middle way

Behavior: temporary nature of a person

Bismillah: a divine phrase of starting something with the blessing of Allah ﷻ

Book of Chant: the Qurãn

Boost: increase

Bowing down: bending one's body, especially the act of respect by bending one's body, for Allah ﷻ

Candy: hard delight, especially in Sufism, the pleasures or miracles given to the person on the path of Allah ﷻ

Caution: carefulness, alertness, especially in Sufism, in spiritual manners not to be trapped by ego or self

Certainty: knowing without doubt, especially in Sufism, knowing and experiencing without doubt

Chanting: repeating, especially in Sufism, repeating the phrases with focus and experience

Chaos: disorder and confusion, especially in Sufism (spiritual) chaos being in negative states of anxiety, stress, and purposelessness

Charge: positive states of spirituality that makes the person happy, peaceful, and calm, especially in Sufism, filling oneself with divine knowledge and experience

Compassion: loving and caring

Confirming Book: the Qurān

Confirming Scripture: the Qurān

Conscience: internal instinct of distinguishing right or wrong

Consciousness: awareness

Constant: not changing, permanent, especially in practice, known as Reflective Attributes of Allah ﷻ, where humans have an image but Allah ﷻ has its source

Construction: formation of an abstract entity

Contract: squeeze

Convergence: similarity

Cookie: soft delight, small sweet cake, especially in Sufism, the pleasures or miracles given to the person on the path of Allah ﷻ

Cosmology: knowledge about the origin and development of the universe

Covenant: agreement

Death: end of physical faculties of a person, especially physical versus spiritual death; the soul does not die but the body dies in understanding of physical death in Islam

Dedication: sincere constant effort

Deity: representation of the transcendent

Detox: discharge

Devout: pious, practicing

Dhikr: as one of the names of the Qurān, or any type of chant to remember Allah ﷻ

Discharge: negative states of spirituality that makes the person sad, stressed, and anxious, especially in Sufism, emptying oneself from all the temporal and worldly positive and negative attachments

Divine: transcendent

Doctrine: teaching

Dominance: control

Dream: visions when one is sleeping or awake

Ego: self, identifier of a person, especially in Sufism, raw and uneducated identifier and controller of a person

Elohim: name of Allah ﷻ in Judaism

Embodiment, versus embody: making it part of one's character

Endeavor: engagement, activities

Epistemology: theory of knowledge

Ethical: moral

Ethnographic: based on observation

Etiquette: good manners and respect, especially in Sufism, respect in the relationship with Allah ﷻ

Evil: anything that causes stress, sadness, or anxiety

Evil eye: the belief of unknown effects of the human eye across different cultures, traditions, and religions, especially in Sufism the evil eye effects due to extreme hatred, jealousy, or, oppositely, evil eye effects due to extreme veneration and love of someone

Expand: enlarge

Experience: internalization of knowledge

Experience or experiential knowledge: all types of learning except from a book or a teacher, internalizing and personalizing the formal learning

Figurative: unclear, secondary, and metaphorical

Free Will: free choice of a person in decision-making

Generous: with capital G, Allah ﷻ

Genre: type

Genuine: sincere, original, authentic

Ghazali: philosopher, theologician, Sufi mystic, lived in 12th century

Glorification: the mental, spiritual, and maybe verbal act of describing Allah ﷻ in an admirable way

Groundless: fake

Habitual: habit of doing something constantly

HasbiyaAllah: a chant with a meaning of "Allah ﷻ is sufficient for me"

Healthy Cookies: beneficial extraordinary incidents, such as miracles in Sufism

Heaven: a place of all maximized pleasures of bodily and spiritual engagements while being with Allah ﷻ

Hell: a place of punishment

Heretic: abnormal person, especially in Sufism, a desired state of being to experience and know the Divine

Humbleness: behavior of modesty in viewing oneself, especially in Sufism, accepting the weakness in one's relationship with Allah ﷻ and not being disrespectful and arrogant to Allah ﷻ

Humility: character or trait of humbleness

Illa Allah: "except Allah" or "except Allah ﷻ"

Images of Allah ﷻ: understandings and experiences about Allah ﷻ

Imitation: trying without real understanding

Infinite: Allah ﷻ, the Unlimited

Informant: a person who participates in anthropological research

InshAllah: Allah ﷻ willing, hopefully

Intention: planning ideas before the action

Internalize: making it part of one's character, trait, or nature in Sufism

Intrinsic: internal

Islam: name of a religion that emphasizes believing in one Allah ﷻ and Jesus, Moses, and Muhammad to be the human prophets of the Creator

Jihad: struggle, esp. spiritual struggle within oneself

Joseph: Prophet of Allah ﷻ in Islam, Christianity, and Judaism

Journey: struggles of following guidelines of a mystical school

Khidr: mystical being who is sent by Allah ﷻ at any time to help people in their problems; also believed to be the teacher of Moses in a mystical journey as mentioned in the Qurãn

Kitab: the Qurãn

Knowledge: theoretical understanding of something through education

La ilaha illa Allah: there is no Allah ﷻ except Allah, a critical Divine phrase of chanting in Sufism implying a spiritual charge and discharge

Literal: clear and primary

Lord: Allah ﷻ

Lucifer: Satan, mentioned in divine Qurãn such as the Bible and the Qurãn

Majnun: crazy or, especially in Sufism, heretic

Mantra: a repetitive phrase or sound, especially used in Hinduism and Buddhism

Meditation: deep focus especially with reflection

Memorization: learning by heart

Mercy: compassion and forgiveness

Middle way: living a balanced life in spiritual and worldly engagements

Mimic: imitate

Mind: logic, reason, and rationality

Miracle: incidents against the law of physics and against all natural sciences

Mosque: temple of Muslims

Muhammad: Rasulullah ﷺ of Islam, referred as "the Prophet" in the text

Musaddiq: the Qurān

Mystic: a person who adopts the teachings of mysticism

Mysticism: the knowledge of the transcendent

Nafs: self in its raw form

Neat: tidy and in order

Negation: denial, esp. in Sufism, emptying from the mind and heart the imperfect ideas and feelings about Allah ﷻ

Neglectful: not giving the proper attention that is due

Notion: concept, idea

Ocean: a very large sea, especially in Sufism, represents Allah ﷻ the Unlimited or Allah ﷻ's Unlimited and Incomprehensible Knowledge

Odd: not even, unique, no equivalence

Olam: hidden, waiting to be discovered through experiential knowledge

One: with capital denoting the one and only Creator

Oppression: unjust action of the strong over the weak

Permanent: constant, not changing, not ending

Phenomenon: occurrence

Pious: devout, practicing

Poisonous Cookies: harmful extraordinary incidents, such as miracles in Sufism

Pollution: making something dirty

Popular culture: the ethnographic data gathered over the period of years among different Sufi communities

Preposition: a word that does not have a meaning by itself but has a meaning in relation to another word, especially in Sufism, prepositions having conceptual and terminological meanings when one describes the relationships with the Divine

Pronunciation: correct sounds of letters in a language

The Prophet: Rasulullah ﷺ *Muhammad (peace and blessings be upon him). The Arabic writing* ﷺ is read as "Sallahu alayhi wa salllam" abbreviated as "saws" when the name of Rasulullah ﷺ Muhammad is mentioned. The expressions ﷺ or saws are expressions and phrases of blessings and peace for Rasulullah ﷺ Muhammad. They are also the expressions and phrases of blessings and peace used for the other Prophets of Allah such as Abraham, Moses, and Jesus and others.

Prostration versus to prostrate: the act of respect by putting one's face on the ground, especially in Sufism, humbling oneself for Allah ﷻ by putting the face, the noble part of the body, on the ground

Qibla: the direction where Muslims and Sufis turn when they pray

Qurãn: sacred text of Muslims

Rabbinic: related with the Rabbis, the priests, and teachers of Judaism
Recitation, versus to recite: reading versus to read

Rasulullah ﷺ: The word Rasulullah can be translated as "the Messenger or Prophet of Allah." Rasulullah in its usage is Rasulullah ﷺ *Muhammad (peace and blessings be upon him)* (PBUH). PBUH: *Peace and blessings be upon Him*

Reliance: dependence

Repetition: repeating

Reverence: respect

Reward: prize, payment, especially in worldly and afterlife rewards in Islam

Ritual: practices in a religion or mysticism that have spiritual and divine value for a person

Ruku: bowing down

Rumi: great Sufi mystic

Saint: the person believed to be close to Allah ﷻ

Sakina: peaceful and calm feelings

Salawat: names of the chants to remember teachers and their covenants with their students, especially the main teacher, Rasulullah ﷺ Muhammad and others, such as Abraham, Moses, and Jesus

Samad: the One who does not need anything, but everyone and everything needs Allah ﷻ

Satan: the Devil, Lucifer, mentioned in divine Qurãn such as in the Bible and the Qurãn

SAW: "Sallahu alayhi wa salllam" abbreviated as "saws" when the name of Rasulullah ﷺ Muhammad is mentioned. The expressions ﷺ or saws are expressions and phrases of blessings and peace for Rasulullah ﷺ Muhammad and other prophets such as Abraham, Moses, Jesus and others.

Scent: perfume, nice smell

Scholar: expert, especially in Sufism, the experts who practice what they teach (alim)

Scripture: sacred book or sacred text

Self: ego, identifier of a person, especially in Sufism, raw and uneducated identifier and controller of a person

Service: ethical action of doing good for others and society

Spiritual Journey: struggles of following guidelines of a mystical school

State: level, especially in Sufism, spiritual level

Struggle: efforts to achieve a goal

SubhanAllah: glorification of Allah ﷻ, a divine phrase of chanting of spirituality implying a spiritual charge and discharge

SubhanAllahu wa bihamdihi: a divine phrase of glorification of Allah ﷻ

SubhanAllahul Azeem: a divine phrase of glorification of Allah ﷻ in the prostration posture

SubhanRabbiyalAzim: phrase of glorification for Allah ﷻ in the bowing posture

Submission: natural acceptance of the uncontrolled and unseen

Sufi: follower of Sufism

Sufism: mystical path of Islam

Superstitious: fake

Surrender: involuntary state of acceptance of the uncontrolled and the unseen

SWT: Subhānahu wa Tā'la also abbreviated as SWT and written as also Allah (ﷻ) is an expression of respect when the Name of Allah is mentioned.

Tahajjud: night prayer

Talismanic: unknown and indescribable effects of divine words and sounds

Taqwa: respect of Allah ﷻ

Taste: pleasure, especially spiritual pleasure such as peace, calmness, joy, and happiness in Sufism

Temple: worship place

Temporal: ending

Temporary: transitory

Temptation: false ideas

The Curer: Allah ﷻ

The Divine: Allah ﷻ

The Forgiver: a name of Allah ﷻ in Sufism

The Friend: a name of Allah ﷻ in Sufism

The Helper: a name of Allah ﷻ in Sufism

The Lover: a name of Allah ﷻ in Sufism

The Peace Giver: Allah ﷻ

The Prophet: Muhammad, Rasulullah ﷺ of Islam, referred as "the Prophet" in the text

The Real: Allah ﷻ

The Real Maker: Allah ﷻ

The Source: Allah ﷻ

The Sustainer: a name of Allah ﷻ in Sufism

The Reminder: the Qurãn

The Wise: with capital W, Allah ﷻ

Throne: a figurative or metaphorical representation of dominion of Allah ﷻ

Trait: permanent character or nature

Tranquility: peace and calmness

Transcendent: beyond human limits

Transitory: temporal

Transliteration: writing the sounds of words or phrases in one language with an alphabet of another language

Union: being together, especially in this book, goal and joy of being always in the presence of Allah ﷻ

Unseen: anything five senses cannot testify in scientific methods

Weak: not having a physical strength to perform an action, especially in Sufism, not having spiritual strength to perform any action

Worshipper: a person who regularly follows and practices rituals, acts of prayers

ACKNOWLEDGMENTS

I would like to thank all my unnamed teachers, friends, and students for their input, ideas, suggestions, help, and support during and before the preparation of this book.

I would like to thank Dr. David Banks, faculty of the Department of Anthropology, State University of New York (SUNY), Sister Toni Hajdaj, Sister Umm Aisha, Dr. AbdulAhad, Br. Ali Rifat and His wife Sister Yildiz at-Turki, Sheikh Dr. Omar of Maryland al-Hindi, Sheikh Tamer of Buffalo, and Sheikh Ali of Hartford Seminary, Sisters Asya Hamad, Amina Osman, and Fatima Samrodia of Darul-Ulum Madania of Buffalo for all their editing, suggestions and comments.

I want to also thank the team of Medina House Publishing in all their preparations and efforts at all stages of this book especially Br. Murat, Br. Khalid (Halit), Br. Mehmet (Matt), Sister Karen, Sister Dorothy-Damla, and Sister Anna Engle.

Lastly, I would like to thank all of my family members for their patience with me during the preparation of this book.

We ask Allah ﷻ to accept all our efforts with the Divine Karam, Fadl, and Grace but not with our faulty and limited efforts deeming rejection. اللَّهُمَّ صلِّ عَلى سَيِّدِناَ وَ حَبِيْبَنَا وَ مَوْلاَناَ مُحَمَّد.

AUTHOR BIO

Dr. M. Yunus Kumek is currently teaching on Muslim Ministry and Spiritual Care at Harvard Divinity School. He has been religious studies coordinator at State University of New York (SUNY) Buffalo State and teaching undergraduate and graduate courses in religious studies at SUNY at Buffalo State, Niagara University and Daemen College. Before becoming interested in religious studies, Dr. Kumek was doing his doctorate degree in physics at SUNY at Buffalo, and had published academic papers in the areas of quantum physics and medical physics. Then, he decided to engage with the world of social sciences through social anthropology, education, and cultural anthropology in his doctorate studies and subsequently, spent a few years as a research associate in the anthropology department of the same university. Recently, he completed a postdoctoral fellowship at Harvard Divinity school and published books on religious literacy through ethnography and selected passages from the Quran with interpreted contextual meanings. Dr. Kumek had classical training in Islamic sciences from the teachers of Egypt, India, Turkey, Yemen, Somalia, Morocco, and the United States. He stayed and studied in Egypt and Turkey. Dr. Kumek, who remains interested in physics—solves physics problems to relax—enjoys different languages: German, Spanish, Arabic, Urdu, and Turkish, especially in his research of scriptural analysis. Dr. Kumek takes great pleasure in classical poetry as well.

SUGGESTED READINGS

Al-Ghazali, M. *Deliverance from Error*. Fons Vitae, 2000.

Al-Ghazali, M. *Ihya 'Ulum al-Din.'* Dar al-Fikr, 2004.

Al-Ghazzali, M. *On the Treatment of Anger, Hatred and Envy*. Kazi Publications, 2003.

Al-Ghazzali, M. *The Alchemy of Happiness*. Routledge, 2015.

Ali, A. Y. *The Meaning of the Glorious Qurān*. Islamic Books, 1938.

Anjum, Z. Iqbal: *The Life of a Poet, Philosopher, and Politician*. Random House, 2015.

Arberry, A. *Interpretation of Koran*. Macmillan, 1955.

Arberry. *Muslim Saints and Mystics: Episodes from Tadhirat al awliya of Faird al-Din Attar, Omphaloskepsis*, 2000.

Asad, M. *The Message of the Qurān: Translated and Explained*. Al-Andalus Gibraltar, 1980.

Avery, K. S. *A Psychology of Early Sufi Sama: Listening and Altered States*. Routledge, 2004.

Awang, R. "Anger Management: A Psychotherapy Sufistic Approach," vol. 9, no. 1, 2014, pp. 13–15.

Barks, C. *Rumi: Bridge to the Soul*. Harperone, 2007.

Barks, R. N. C. with J. Moyne, Rumi, Jelaluddin. "The guest house." *The Essential Rumi*. Harper, 1995, p. 109.

Bayrak, T. *The Name & the Named*. Canada, 2000.

Berguno, G. & Loutfy, N. "The Existential Thoughts of the Sufis. Existential Analysis." *Journal of the Society for Existential Analysis*, vol. 16, no. 1, 2005.

Bowen, J. *A New Anthropology of Islam*. Cambridge University Press, 2012.

Clarke, M. "Cough Sweets and Angels: The Ordinary Ethics of the Extraordinary in Sufi Practice in Lebanon." *Journal of the Royal Anthropological Institute*, vol. 20, no. 3, 2014, pp. 407–25.

Cutsinger, J. S. *Paths to the Heart*. World Wisdom, 2010.

Douglas-Klotz, N. *The Sufi Book of Life: 99 Pathways of the Heart for the Modern Dervish*. Penguin, 2005.

Ernst, C. W. *Teachings of Sufism*. Shambhala Publications, 1999.

Esposito, J. *The Oxford Dictionary of Islam*. Oxford University Press, 2014.

Friedlander, S. *The Whirling Dervishes: Being an Account of the Sufi Order Known as the Mevlevis and its Founder the Poet and Mystic Mevlana Jalalu'ddin Rumi*. SUNY Press, 1975.

Geoffroy, E. *Introduction to Sufism: The Inner Path of Islam*. World Wisdom, Inc., 2010.

Gibran, K. *The Prophet*. Oneworld Publications, 2012.

Hanson, Y. H. "The Creed of Imam Al-Tahawi." Zaytuna Institute, California, 2007.

Hanson, Y. H. *Purification of the Heart*. Alhambra Productions, 1998.

Helminski, K. *The Knowing Heart: A Sufi Path of Transformation*. Shambhala Publications, 2000.

Izutsu, T. *Sufism and Taoism: A Comparative Study of Key Philosophical Concepts*. University of California Press, 2016.

James, W. "The Will to Believe." *New World*, 1896.

Jawziyyah, Q. *The Prophetic Medical Science*. Idara Impex, 2013.

Karamustafa, T. A. *Sufism*. Edinburgh University Press, 2007.

Katz, J. G. "Dreams, Sufism, and Sainthood." *Brill,* vol. 71, 1996.

Khan, Z. M. *Gardens of the Righteous*. Routledge, 2012.

Lewis, B. *Music of a Distant Drum: Classical Arabic, Persian, Turkish, and Hebrew Poems*. Princeton University Press, 2001.

Malak, A. *Muslim Narratives and the Discourse of English*. SUNY Press, 2007.

Morris, J. W. "Introducing Ibn 'Arabī's Book of Spiritual Advice." *Journal of the Muhyiddīn Ibn 'Arabī Society,* no. 28, 2000, pp. 1–17.

Pickthall, M. W. E. *Holy Qurān*. Kutub Khana Isha'at-ul-Islam, 1977.

Ramji, R. *The Global Migration of Sufi Islam to South Asia and Beyond*. Brill, 2007, pp. 473–84.

Renard J. *Knowledge of Allah ﷻ in Classical Sufism: Foundations of Islamic Mystical Theology*. Paulist Press, 2004.

Rumi, J. *The Essential Rumi*. Harper, 1996.

Schimmel, A. *Deciphering the Signs of Allah ﷻ: A Phenomenological Approach to Islam.* State University of New York Press, 1994.

Siddiqui, A. "Sahih Muslim." *Peace Vision,* 1972.

Trimingham, J. S. *The Sufi Orders in Islam.* Oxford University Press, 1998.

Upton, C. *Doorkeeper of the Heart: Versions of Rabi'a.* Threshold Books, 1988.

Usmani, T. *An Approach to the Qur'anic Sciences.* Adam Publishers, 2006.

INDEX

www.ingramcontent.com/pod-product-compliance
Lightning Source LLC
Chambersburg PA
CBHW071707030726
47598CB00013B/2440